THE PHILOSOPHY OF GESTURE

I0895571

# The Philosophy of Gesture

## Completing Pragmatists' Incomplete Revolution

GIOVANNI MADDALENA

McGill-Queen's University Press
Montreal & Kingston · London · Chicago

© McGill-Queen's University Press 2015

ISBN 978-0-7735-4612-7 (cloth)
ISBN 978-0-7735-4613-4 (paper)
ISBN 978-0-7735-9788-4 (ePDF)
ISBN 978-0-7735-9789-1 (ePUB)

Legal deposit fourth quarter 2015

Bibliothèque nationale du Québec

Printed in Canada on acid-free paper that is 100% ancient forest free (100% post-consumer recycled), processed chlorine free

Publication of this book has been supported by grants from the University of Molise and Difendiamo il futuro.

McGill-Queen's University Press acknowledges the support of the Canada Council for the Arts for our publishing program. We also acknowledge the financial support of the Government of Canada through the Canada Book Fund for our publishing activities.

---

Library and Archives Canada Cataloguing in Publication

Maddalena, Giovanni, 1971-, author
The philosophy of gesture : completing pragmatists' incomplete revolution / Giovanni Maddalena.

Includes bibliographical references and index.
Issued in print and electronic formats.
ISBN 978-0-7735-4612-7 (bound). – ISBN 978-0-7735-4613-4 (paperback). – ISBN 978-0-7735-9788-4 (ePDF). – ISBN 978-0-7735-9789-1 (ePUB)

1. Pragmatism. 2. Identity (Philosophical concept). 3. Act (Philosophy). I. Title.

B832.M14 2015 144'.3 C2015-904763-3
C2015-904764-1

*To my friends who suffer.*
*Freedom is a complete gesture as well.*

Crystal clearness, such as we justly require in mathematics, in law, in economics, is in philosophy the characteristic of the second rates. The reason is that the strongest men are able to seize an all-important conception long before the progress of analysis has rendered it possible to free it from obscurities and difficulties.

C.S. Peirce, *Contributions to The Nation* 2, 84, 1894

# Contents

# Foreword

**FERNANDO ZALAMEA**
Universidad Nacional de Colombia

Since Greek times, philosophy has always been attentive to surprise, novelty, and originality, hoping to offer a better understanding of the world thanks to the use of new perspectives, both sensible and intelligible. On the other hand, a fine appraisal of the practice of gestures provides a welcome bridge between the two main rationales of intelligence: heart and reason. Giovanni Maddalena's *The Philosophy of Gesture* thus enters at the very core of the most crucial problems of philosophy, and, for that matter, of mathematics (through Grothendieck's yin-yang geometrization), music (through Mazzola's ongoing gesture theory), art (through Kiefer's installations), or literature (through Valéry's exploration of inventiveness in the *Cahiers*). The main appeal of Maddalena's book comes from his effort to look at a philosophically central issue from its borders, using non-standard, alternative tools of thought: a profusion of synthetic patterns, an understanding of the topological logic of Peirce's existential graphs, a look to Grossman's literature, and a personal, wonderfully innovative (and may I say, Italian) blend of semiotics, phenomenology, and metaphysics. *Freshness – Plasticity – Life.* If we later point out the many new treatments in Maddalena's book, we certainly have first to thank him for the freshness that *The Philosophy of Gesture* provides in the often-sclerotic land of "academic philosophy."

In chapter 1, Maddalena situates the debate Kantianism/anti-Kantianism, and explains how Peirce's pragmatism leads to a sound middle way between the opposites. Developing a study of signs, continuity, and common sense, Maddalena introduces a philosophy of gesture as an "attempt to foster pragmatist insight toward a closer unification of experience and methods of inquiry." The apparent contradiction between analysis (on the side of intelligible inquiry) and synthesis (on the side of sensible unification of experience) comes thus as a central problem to be explored. Maddalena presents, first, a closer look to synthetic patterns (chapter 2, following Peirce; to be supplemented, in chapter 3, with a profound analysis of Peirce's existential graphs) and, second, he imagines the way to new, working definitions of analysis and synthesis (chapter 3, "a new paradigm for reasoning"). This is a truly revolutionary path, where Maddalena *characterizes* each form of reasoning according to the behavior of the changes (actions, gestures) it produces in identity: analysis recognizing identity through changes, synthesis losing identity through changes, and vagueness (a third way) being blind to identity through changes. Chapter 3 produces additional arguments (mathematical gestures, logical modalities, Peirce's continuum) in order to explain the core of the new definitions, and their eventual applicability in philosophy.

After opening new grounds and perspectives for synthetic reasoning, Maddalena focuses in chapter 4 on the eventual uses of universals in singulars, moments where some kind of "perfection" (either semiotic or mathematical) appears. He then introduces "a new tool: complete gesture" to explain the richness of those flashes of inquiry where pragmatism, semiotics, and mathematics concur. A thorough analysis of complete and incomplete gestures shows them as counterparts of logical and epistemic analysis. Maddalena's *moving methodology* (both dynamic and emotional, letting surface Maddalena's truly great power as an essayist, in the best Italian tradition) emerges here at his very best, applying analytical tools to the understanding of synthesis, synthesizing the intermediate conclusions obtained, and always situating himself at the borders and superpositions of alternative perspectives. Chapter 5 applies the ideas introduced in the previous chapters to an understanding of creativity in a wide sense. Overcoming dichotomies, a study of pragmatist aesthetics (Margolis, Shusterman) is seen as a necessary counterpart to analytical reasoning, and Maddalena attempts to explain creativity through a very original study of existential graphs and complete gestures. A final section of chapter 5 elaborates on "conditions of creativity" (with wonderful literary examples in Tolkien and Melville), where some connections with Maddalena's previous works on ethics and normativity are explored.

Chapter 6 ("Figural and Narrative Identity") and chapter 7 ("Writing as Complete Gesture") become truly *plastic* consequences and examples of the ideas, theories, and methods advanced in the book. Again, some sort of Gödelian self-reference (a *diagonal* method applied to itself) is at work, enriching both the text and its many interpretations. Maddalena's natural literary talent (both as a theatre writer and as an essayist) *frees* itself from the usual straitjackets of academic philosophy, with studies of "continuity of narration," "identity and memory," and "literary self-reflection," alongside fine revisions of Homer, the Gospels, Auerbach, Tolkien, or Grossman (a dense chapter 7 is devoted to *Life and Fate*, as a major example of complete gesture). A final chapter 8 tackles questions on morality and education from the viewpoint of the advocated philosophy of gesture. Here one can see the young scholar truly moved by life itself, longing for a better practice of human kindness, along a spiritual path that Maddalena also explores in his daily behaviour through his religious convictions. Peircean at heart, Maddalena combines all experiences of human knowledge and sensitivity, either mathematical, philosophical, semiotic, ethical, mystic, or literary. The complete panorama of human endeavor is pursued by a true visionary, who hopes to encode parts of it in complete gestures. As Borges would tell us, the venture is necessarily doomed to fail, but the essential action consists in trying to produce the code: Maddalena's very attempt is a new form of knowledge on which further roads will be built.

Beyond the many original views presented in *The Philosophy of Gesture*, the book is in fact particularly valuable for the open questions it offers to the reader. A section on "Conclusions and Further Studies" reinforces such venues, which in fact were hinted at all along the book. Compared with the extraordinary development of analytical philosophy in the twentieth century, what one may call a "synthetic," complementary approach is still in its infancy, despite a Peirce, a Florensky, a Grothendieck. Maddalena's text underlines the importance of searching for a new paradigm for the polarity analysis/synthesis, which the Italian scholar resolves through his new approach related to a central dialectics in knowledge: change and identity. Maddalena's definition and development of complete gestures, and their application to the understanding of literary narratives, are unprecedented contributions to the (thankfully) blurring intersection of mathematics, phenomenology, semiotics, and literature. In fact, knowledge needs to enter, with new tools and with a brave disposition, the muddy space of real life, far away from the supposedly crystalline waters of analytic philosophy. As a third way, beyond analysis and synthesis, Maddalena mentions the need to construct a *horotics* (following Roberto Perry), a systematic study of the borders and frontiers between the traditional opposites. Another fascinating path will be the elaboration of some sort of *a posteriori metaphysics*, a wonderful contradiction on which Maddalena has been thinking since his previous book (*Metafisica per assurdo*, 2009).

Logics are changing (beyond classical logic, intermediate categorical logic, the logic of sheaves, and the logic of paraconsistency allow us to understand better the idea of creative, partial contradictions) and our very ideas of number and space (through Grothendieck's revolution: schemes and topos) should quickly transform our usual, rather static forms of knowledge. In that evolving, dynamic world which has long affected mathematics, semiotics, and literature, Maddalena's *The Philosophy of Gesture* will be considered in the future, with due perspective, as an important contribution that will have opened in turn the more conservative bunker of philosophy.

THE PHILOSOPHY OF GESTURE

# Introduction

## THE SYNTHETIC DRIVE OF PRAGMATISM

Long since Immanuel Kant wrote the *Critique of Pure Reason*, the real watershed of modernity, philosophers have tried either to complete his critical project or to reject it. Even more than René Descartes, Kant compelled future philosophers to take radical standings, whether for or against his own. This is because Kant's project reflects and gives form to the entire mentality of the contemporary world. Kant was right in saying that his critical assessment was a Copernican revolution. In comparison, Descartes' revolution simply ameliorated the old scholastic tradition to which it was opposed. As a matter of fact, many thinkers have shown that Descartes is ambiguous even in rejecting scholasticism. You can still read his work as a completion of what was said before him.[1] One can take him as really reassessing the scholastic tradition in new ways. You cannot do the same with Kant; when the Copernican revolution started, modernity took its contemporary form. Kant's is not an amelioration, but instead a coup d'état on philosophical mentality and reasoning. This book aims to provide a pragmatist alternative to some crucial aspects of Kant's philosophy. This alternative has not been explored yet within the contemporary philosophical landscape, not even by classic pragmatists who often involuntarily accepted aspects of Kant's legacy.

In fact, we can even trace the history of contemporary philosophy from Kant. Both analytic and continental philosophies – as much as this distinction still makes sense – derived their form from

Kant's project. In a way both are realizations or completions of Kant's thought. Analytic philosophy took seriously the distinction between analytic and synthetic reasoning and judgment, conferring to the first a supremacy that tried either to swallow the second or to abandon it to "useless" realms like ethics, aesthetics, politics, or religion. After this, analytic philosophy took on a more complex pattern but – as the name still indicates – its reliance upon analysis remained a fundamental characteristic. True enough, there were strong critiques of the synthetic-analytic distinction from W.V.O. Quine onward (1951),[2] but they were internal to the same tradition. Fortunately they weakened the absolutism of the first phase, but they did not overturn the deep Kantian insight that was at the root of this model of philosophy.

Phenomenology and hermeneutics tried a different method that I still consider to be Kantian. They took the subjective turn of Kantian revolution so seriously that they risked solipsism or positive arbitrarism. Both philosophies attacked Kant many times from different points of view, but I fear they unwillingly stuck to his project. Edmund Husserl's project remained analytic. He tried an analysis of our phenomenological approach to reality and, in the *Cartesian Meditations* (1931), he even leaned toward a solipsistic turn. On the other hand, hermeneutics has often relied upon an interpretation of the transcendental philosophy filtered through German idealism and its Kantian heritage. Even if singular points of Kant's work were criticized or overturned, the general pattern of his philosophy holds even now in our philosophical mentality and in our common sense.

What is still standing of that project? What are the points that a new proposal should tackle? Kant's philosophy permeates the philosophies that follow him in many ways, but there are three results that are particularly relevant to what I want to propose.

The first effect of Kant's legacy is the general notion of reason that relies upon a certain conception of necessity. As much as Kant strived to reach an ampliative view of reason and reasoning that could account for our synthetic capacity in reading or constructing reality, he always grounded his speculative building on a rationalist pattern of necessity composed by the hierarchical relationship between parts and whole. I hope to show precisely how this pattern underlies Kant's project in chapter 3. For now I will limit myself to saying that this pattern produces a view of reason typical of the Enlightenment, according to which reason is the "measure of all things" even though this measure greatly differs from the Protagorean, utilitarian version of it.[3] Kant is not utilitarian at all. Reason encircles what we call experience so that nothing can escape it, but within that circle reason has to find an account of every phenomenon, beyond any consideration of utility. This picture of reason has remained in every type of subsequent philosophy. Setting aside the complex discourses on idealism in general, and on G.W.F. Hegel in particular, let us say that in the twentieth century reason has still been connected with necessity and with a rationalist kind of explanation. The only difference was that either this explanation was reduced to certain fields (neo-positivism) or it was rejected as a tragic outcome of a progressively technological possession of Being, as in a certain hermeneutics derived from Heidegger.

Phenomenologists or pragmatists took themselves beyond Kant's philosophy but assumed an underlying scheme of necessity: at the end they would always find themselves searching for the exact components of the "whole" of knowledge. C.S. Peirce himself ended up adopting some of Kant's assumptions, even though he was perhaps more astute in identifying the rationalist trouble when he pointed out that reasoning is not like a chain, whose power depends upon its weakest ring, but like a rope, whose robustness depends upon unity among many different threads (*EP1*, 29). Unfortunately he could not hold this view to its foremost conclusion, as we are going to see throughout the second chapter.[4] However, his statements outline the basic point of the change in our conception of reason that this book hopes to foster.

The second effect of the Kantian legacy that the new proposal has to consider is the view of morality. Kant makes some self-consistent autonomy the centrepiece of his moral theory. The idea that true morals should be autonomously held is part of the general way in which we conceive the world. From newspapers and TV shows to private judgments on ourselves, morality has become moralism. What is moralism? Moralism consists in deciding on a value, in believing in it as in a God – the Bible called it an idol – and then to sacrifice ourselves with any effort in order to realize it, measuring ourselves and others according to the enslaving rules that precipitate from it. Values become idols and idols ideologies. The transformation of values into idols and idols into ideologies has occurred in this past century in the form of various totalitarian governments. But such a transformation can happen in any individual life. One can be ideological in his/her job, faith, community, or family. Eighteenth-century society was ideological and moralistic about sex exactly as our society is ideological about honesty, individual rights and health.

What is the link between pure Kantian morality and ideology, and, even less clearly, totalitarianism? Kant's morality abandons the complex view of reality held by the moral realist in favour of an intellectualist and self-centred conception of reality based on inner determination and effort. Once the moral realist view of reality is abandoned, and also heteronomy with its typical balance between different values, the groundless tenacity of ideologies takes over and is fostered by steady guardians. One can be very moral and dutiful in helping any killing machine that satisfies his/her own intellectual principles (Arendt 1963). It is certainly possible to trace this attitude toward morality even in Greek intellectualism from Socrates on, but it never was so powerful as when allied with Kant's Copernican revolution on knowledge. Given the general picture of knowledge of the *Critique of Pure Reason*, intellectualist moralism acquired an immense power. Much more than John Rawls' reformulation or Jürgen Habermas' contemporary critical translation, morality as conceived by Kant deeply influences everyday mentality.

The last effect of Kant's legacy is visible in the separations that now exist between fields of inquiry and among disciplines. The notorious gap between sciences and humanities that so deeply affects Western culture – with profound inconveniences, above all in this time of economic and social crisis when we need a creative, unitary mentality – is largely due to the critical system that Kant proposed with enormous success. Certainly this gap was fostered and helped by subsequent idealism and positivism in the nineteenth century, and by hermeneutics, existentialism, and neo-positivism during the twentieth century. Again, it is Kant's Copernican revolution and conception of pure reason that lies beneath this overall picture of knowledge. Also, the rehabilitation of practical philosophy in its many shapes does not happen outside of Kant's picture of knowledge. The rehabilitation of *phronesis* against *episteme* accepts that episteme is not practical knowledge, confirming the chasm between theoretical and practical realms that Kant consecrated.[5]

I will not analyze the many traditions of philosophy according to a Kantian/anti-Kantian perspective. In this book I will show how pragmatism, understood in a certain way, suggests a different view that overhauls these three effects of Kant's legacy. The aim of this book then is similar to that of Richard Rorty, who was committed to the same task in his *Philosophy and the Mirror of Nature* (1979) and in *Consequences of Pragmatism* (1982). He correctly identified Kant as the polemic adversary of pragmatism, but he failed to understand the real reason for this. Rorty thought that the problem with Kant was in his theory of representation, the last outcome of a metaphysical foundational tradition. So deep was Rorty's belief that he excluded Peirce's seminal work from his narration of the history of pragmatism. According to him, Peirce was too much affected by Kant's views about knowledge (1982, 161). Peirce based his conception of knowledge on a theory of representation, and according to Rorty's standards this attitude could not be pragmatist at all. Curiously, Rorty's way of proposing pragmatism as an alternative to Kant required that he rejected Peirce as pragmatism's founding father. If he had cared a little more for historical and philological accounts, he would have noticed that Peirce himself was much more anti-Kantian than he is usually taken to be and his theory of representation was very different from Kant's. I will address this attitude of Peirce and pragmatists toward Kant in the first chapter. This different approach to the relationship between Peirce and Kant will lead to a conclusion far from Rorty's. The point is not "to get away from the notion of 'an account of human knowledge'" (Rorty 1979, 180) but to give an account that is not tied to a conception of representation as a mirror, which Rorty accuses Peirce of. Rorty's refusal of the Kantian tradition correctly takes both phenomenology and analytic philosophy to fall short of creative counter-proposals. Without a third alternative, Rorty's refusal of Kantian philosophy leads him to a behaviouristic view that does not respect either the privileged epistemologies that he despises or the common sense that pragmatism has always defended.

Paradoxically, Peirce himself is the starting point of a new alternative to Kantianism. Contrary to many surveys of Peirce's philosophy, I read Peirce's work as a clear departure from Kant. He progressively took his independence from Kant on the first point of our summary of Kant's legacy: the conception of reason. Recent studies show that young Peirce understood Kant in an unorthodox way (Chevalier 2013). In any case, in his mature manuscripts Peirce abandoned Kantianism in the name of a strong scholastic realism. This rejection of Kantianism and the adherence to metaphysical realism appear more evidently on a cosmological and metaphysical level. These epistemic roots are to be found in Peirce's lifelong striving for a new understanding of synthetic reasoning that had two features: 1) synthetic reasoning could not be a mere reversal of analytic judgment and 2) it had to be completely different from that synthetic apperception that Kant placed at the base of his theoretical building. Peirce worked on the possibility of a different understanding of synthesis, from his early studies on hypothesis and induction until his mature formulations of abduction and existential graphs. Not by chance, he identified the graphs as his "chef d'oeuvre." Much more than their functionality, the importance of existential graphs lies in their representation of the process of reasoning. I will show that in the end, Peirce remained fascinated by the formal analytic working of the graphs without trying to understand the real, everyday way in which this synthetic reasoning happens. He was looking for a synthetic turn that remained incomplete in his work, as it did in the work of other pragmatists, as I will maintain in chapters 2 and 3.

From here onward, my journey has to take a new pragmatist path. A different paradigm of synthesis must be proposed. Thanks to studies conducted in cooperation with Fernando Zalamea, the great Colombian essayist and thinker, I will usher in a new philosophical paradigm drawn from Peirce's insights on continuity and existential graphs. In this new light, synthetic reasoning is described as "recognition of identity through change" (ch. 3). I will find a complete synthetic embodiment in a kind of act that I will name "complete gesture" (ch. 4). Gestures are the ordinary way in which we carry on meaning, as the etymology of the word (from *gero* = I bear, I carry on) implies. Complete gestures are those in which new meaning is synthetically acquired. The complexity of gestures will be explained through semiotic tools that Peirce himself discovered. From a pragmatist point of view, the proposal of complete gesture meets and supplements the works of John Dewey (1934) and George H. Mead (1934), thus falling entirely within classical pragmatism.

Once the notion of complete gesture is introduced in chapter 4, I turn to the application of this new tool. Specifically, I apply this notion to several complex issues in modern philosophy, hoping to fill in the blanks left by the Kantian framework on our culture. In particular, I apply the notion of complete gesture to the topics of identity, creativity, morality, and education. These applications will vindicate the importance of complete gesture and – I hope – introduce a fruitful instrument into our philosophical landscape.

Besides Fernando Zalamea and André De Tienne, veritable philosophical *startsy* whose ideas are continuously referenced throughout the whole book, there are people who contributed to the project of this book at various levels: Rosa Maria Calcaterra from a philosophical standpoint, and David Agler, Julie Lasher, Diana Reynolds, and Marco Stango from a linguistic standpoint. I thank also all friends, students, and colleagues who helped by criticizing my ideas during public or private conversations. Among them I want to remember here Guido Baggio, Pier Paolo Bellini, Elisabetta Bruno, Daniel Cefai, Vincent Colapietro, Vincenzo Costa, Rossella Fabbrichesi, Fabio Ferrucci, Barbara Formis, Alessandro Fornero (author of the graphic for figure 4.1 and 4.2), Roberto Frega, Guido Gili, Mathias Girel, Anthony Graybosch, Roberto Gronda, Robert Innis, James Liszka, Joe Margolis, Mario Mascilongo, Juliana Perez, and Lorenzo Scillitani.

# 1

# Anti-Kantianism and Pragmatist Characteristics

## 1. ANTI-KANTIANISM

Pragmatism is one of the few early twentieth-century philosophical movements that are still vital. Unlike other movements, it has not been reduced to a mere historiographical study of the philosophical expressions of a distant age and culture. Much of the current use of the term "pragmatism" is due to Rorty's and Hilary Putnam's revival of it during the 1970s and 1980s, which ensured its availability when hermeneutics and analytical philosophy began to recognize their limits and insurmountable difficulties.[1] Before their recovery of the term, pragmatism was studied and residually preserved by a few universities and scholars, but it remained foreign to mainstream contemporary philosophy.[2] Putnam's and Rorty's revival, though deliberately partial and questionable – especially the latter's – had the merit of reintroducing classic American pragmatism as a viable alternative to the mainstream movements in crisis, or at the very least, as useful material for the restoration of their architectures, which had been shaken by self-criticism.

In this sense, it is perhaps worth trying to regain the trait of anti-Kantianism, which was common among classic pragmatists notwithstanding the different ways they went about it. Much has been rightly said about pragmatists' antagonism towards Descartes and Cartesianism, but perhaps the critique will become more significant when it is joined with anti-Kantianism. Of course, much has also been said about that,[3] especially with regard to William

James.[4] However, criticism often stops at a superficial level, and hardly ever manages to grasp the unity of the phenomenon – above all because of Peirce's initial appreciation of Kant.[5]

Pragmatists' anti-Cartesianism had already been defined in the first appearance of pragmatism, in Peirce's cognition series written for the "Journal of Speculative Philosophy" (1867–68). As is well known, the brilliant young scientist stigmatized the Cartesian doubt as a "paper doubt," by opposing it to the scientists' true "living doubt" (*EP1*, 115). Sometimes readers do not realize the powerful novelty that this opposition implies. According to Peirce, research does not move from the skeptical doubt, which falls under the heading of "paper doubt." More similarly to Augustine,[6] Peirce describes a situation in which you can doubt because you have a previous certainty. Therefore, research moves from one certainty to another certainty, and the abandonment of a first certainty is only due to the occurrence of a real surprising phenomenon that alters one of the pillars on which it stands. Peirce never abandoned this position, even when he corrected the psychologism of his first approach – which paired certainty with satisfaction – toward a realistic direction; he even translated it into a logical pattern when he inserted the "surprising phenomenon" as an actual internal step of the logic of abduction (hypothesis).[7] In these founding papers, intuitionism and introspectivism also ended up in the enemies list with the "paper doubt." In opposition to Descartes, Peirce refused any form of intellectualism and all pragmatism moves in this vein.

However, this argument is still insufficient. Empiricists, existentialists, and hermeneuticians were also anti-Cartesians. Pragmatism clarifies the attack on Descartes with the one on Kant. This second feature has always been overshadowed, primarily because of Peirce. In fact, the founder of pragmatism referred to the *Critique of Pure Reason* as the tables "brought down from Sinai" (*CP* 4.2). He gave a name taken from the German thinker to his doctrine (*CP* 5.412), insisting that the Kantian problem of unity of the manifold was the true issue of epistemology (*EP1*, 1). However, over the years, Peirce emphasized his criticisms more and more, particularly in light of the deepening of his idea of "continuity," the true keystone of his philosophy. He changed his mind on this topic, gradually passing from his original Kantian setting into a Cantorian version. Afterward, thanks to the discovery of Georg Cantor's theorem and paradox (made independently of the German mathematician), he preferred a unique view that places real continuity beyond any logical or metric calculation.[8]

The concept of continuity, and Kant's misconception of it, allowed Peirce to understand why in Kant's thought there is always a "gap" between knowledge and the reality to be known, between the "thing-in-itself" and the "phenomenon." The distinction had troubled him since his early philosophical studies (*W1*, 37–44). During the last twenty years of his life, Peirce considered the permanence of this schism to be the epiphenomenon of an entire intellectual attitude: nominalism, understood here in a very different way from a mere denial of the existence of universals. It can be believed that universals are real, yet one is still nominalist if he/she thinks that universals are hopelessly beyond the inferential capacities of humankind. Nominalism affirms an unbridgeable gap between reality and reason. In this view realism maintains that reason belongs to reality and in the long run of inquiry, it will (or would) know reality.

Peirce adds a second criticism to the one against nominalism; we find it only in a few fragments, but it aligns quite easily with his general approach. In a 1909 manuscript, Peirce writes:

> There is a celebrated passage in the second edition of the *Critick der Reinen Vernunft* and a very notable one, in which Kant says that the "I think" – Das Ich Denke – must be able to accompany all his ideas, "since otherwise they would not thoroughly belong to me." A man less given to discoursing might remark on reading this: "For my part, I don't hold my ideas as my ownty-downty; I had rather they were Nature's and belonged to Nature's author." However, that would be to misinterpret Kant. In his first edition, he does not call the act "the I think" but "the object=x." That which that act has to effect is the consecution of ideas; now, the need of consecution of ideas is a logical need and is due not, as Kant thinks, to their

> taking the form of the Urtheil, the assertion, but to their making an argument; and this is not "I think" that that always virtually accompanies an argument, but it is: "Don't you think so?" (*MS* 636, 1910, 24–6)[9]

In this passage Peirce does not become a defender of the "thing-in-itself" but of the transcendental unity of the object, which if recognized would have led Kant to a realist basis. This is the possibility that Peirce recognizes when he accepts that his doctrine implies objective idealism (*CP* 6.163), although he does not agree with the intellectualism of Hegelian dialectic; Hegel misses what Peirce calls Firstness and Secondness, that is to say the spontaneity of events and their brute occurrence (*EP2*, 177). But at least Hegel understood that the relationship between reality and the human mind must be a profound continuity.

In the same manuscript we find the third criticism: the "I think" does not guarantee the unity of the object because of the aforementioned lack of continuity between cognitive processes and reality. On the contrary, in presuming to unify a scattered reality, it paradoxically becomes presumptuously omnipotent. The "I think" pretends to reunite knowledge with its object and therefore it assumes an ability that is not its responsibility. Peirce, who considered the "I" as a semiotic effect more than a cause (De Tienne 2005, 98), cannot be but ironic about such a hypertrophic view.

Summing up, there are three attacks: nominalism in the specified meaning above, the weakness of the "I think," and the assumptions of this view of the Self that serves as a prelude to the solipsism of certain idealism. These three arguments against Kant's philosophy bear the unmistakable label of pragmatism. A fourth one is often added: the unity of knowledge. Aesthetics and ethics are not separated from the theorizing of logic; on the contrary, in Peirce's classification of sciences they offer the principles on which logic moves forward (*EP2*, 258–62).

All classic pragmatists on both sides of the Atlantic Ocean share Peirce's criticisms. As summarized by J.S. Johnston, throughout his career Dewey retained a criticism similar to Peirce's against Kant.

However, Caird's idealist mediation did not let Dewey appreciate the difference between the transcendental object of the first edition of the *Critique of Pure Reason* and the noumenon of the second. Peirce had praised the former and attacked the latter. Dewey instead considered them identical and submitted them to the critiques of every dualism: the distinction noumenon-phenomenon leaves a gap between the real and the ideal (Johnston 2006, 528).[10] Dewey added a criticism of the weakness of the "I think" as the unifying principle of experience, which is unified only intellectually and formalistically, devoid of any content. Years later Dewey added a further accusation of dualism between nature and morality to these juvenile criticisms borrowed from Hegel, and he even ascribed the imperialist spirit of Germany to this dualism and not – as is more usual among scholars – to an interpretation of Hegel's idealism (Johnston 2006, 537).

Dewey was Peirce's student at Johns Hopkins University in 1882, and it is possible that he borrowed criticisms from him – although we do not know for certain. However, leaving aside this historiographical issue, it is possible to find in Dewey the same criticisms we found with the founder of American pragmatism. The weakness of "the thing-in-itself" criticism in Dewey (the confusion between transcendental object and noumenon) is counterbalanced by a greater awareness of the separation of morality from the knowledge of "nature."

James' criticism is based on the same elements; his felicitous pen became merciless when he supported the need to "circumvent" Kant's philosophy in his article "The Pragmatic Method" – and even to "do without him," because he "bequeaths to us not one single conception which is both indispensable to philosophy and which philosophy either did not possess before him or was not destined inevitably to acquire" (James 1904, 687). With little more thoughtfulness James' *Pragmatism* accuses Kant of intellectualizing experience, which does not offer itself according to the measurements of time and space, understood as intuitions of the intellect in Kant's terminology. "Everything that happens to us brings its own duration and extension, and both are vaguely surrounded by a marginal 'more' that runs into the duration and extension of the next thing that comes ... The great majority of the human race never uses these notions, but lives in plural times and spaces, interpenetrant and *durcheinander*." (James 1907, 177–8). According to James' *Varieties* (1902, 350–1), the complete intellectualization of experience – beginning with those of space and time – is the result of the transcendental doctrine of apperception, mediated by the idealist principles of logic and dialectics. The "I think" is the point disputed in this case as the source of abstraction and the origin of Hegelian idealism, whose rationalist monism James opposed in all his works. On the contrary James thought that his own "radical empiricism" – though originally a monism – could be developed pluralistically.

James rejects, as Dewey does, the "thing-in-itself" as a symbol of the eternal abyss between knowledge and reality. As previously said, it is a dualism to which intellect provides its weak unity. This does not mean that pragmatists do not recognize categories, but that they are not "fulminated before Nature began" and "gradually forming themselves in Nature's presence" (James 1907, 249).

In *A Pluralistic Universe*, in the chapter on Bergson[11] James summarizes his two criticisms in a single statement: "the thing-in-itself" is unintelligible to our minds and that is why appearances can be organized and manipulated by intellect itself. But, given the assumption of unintelligibility, the intellect determines a contradiction that is revealed by the paradoxes of continuity. If the mind can calculate everything indefinitely, does this not contradict the concept of infinite numbers in itself? (James 1909, 238) More fundamentally this means: what unifies the mind if "the thing-in-itself" is unattainable by definition?

James also added a distinctive religious grain to these criticisms. The idealists to whom he was harshly opposed had a principle of unity opposite to that of "the thing-in-itself," in the future and not in the past, and in fact their Absolute derives from the "ego of apperception" and not from Kant's dualist theology. This means that the Absolute is intellectualist because it derives from Kant's intellectualist philosophy, which has little to do with what is authentically religious, even in the German thinker.

Mead's critique starts with morality but focuses on the same elements we have seen in the other pragmatists. According to George Herbert Mead in *Movements of Thought in the Nineteenth Century* (1936, 25–50), Kant's fundamental interest is to affirm the ruling role of human power into society. Kant obtains this goal by the universalizing rule of human will (ibid., 30–1). Kant's example about the maxim of never lying should be taken as the paradigm of this moral pattern. Unfortunately, "Kant did not succeed in that [the general goal]. He did not succeed even with reference to lying. There are many situations in which lying is not immoral" (ibid., 28).

This lawgiving attitude also extends into the field of nature. For Mead, the aim of the *Critique of Pure Reason* is to affirm that "man gives laws to nature" (ibid., 31). As all other pragmatists do, Mead underlines the paradox of this critique of experience that finds the unity of experience itself only in the "ponderous construction" of "the transcendental a priori unity of apperception" (ibid., 45). This somehow organizes what comes from the thing-in-itself understood as another reality, which is the condition of our actual experience (ibid., 46). Mead concludes that we can have some experience because we postulate something that is beyond experience. The phenomenal experience always "implies something beyond itself of which it is the appearance ... But of what it is the appearance we can never know. We cannot even know that there is anything there. We can postulate it but we cannot know" (ibid., 48). Once again the thing in itself, the formality of the "I think," and its tremendous transformation in the moral ruler are questioned. The ponderous construction and its postulates want to overcome David Hume's skepticism finding necessity and universality. However, the concrete experience of science does not find this sort of universality as the discovery of non-Euclidean geometries shows (ibid., 38–40). We are not severed from reality so that we have to be either masters (as Kant wants us to be) or servants (as the traditional metaphysics wants). Mead sees knowledge as a complex interaction. Experience is not a fixed object but a cluster of processes and problems that we have to solve.

The European pragmatists demonstrated a similar attitude toward Kant. The unity of sciences is one of Giovanni Vailati's starting points on anti-Kantianism.[12] According to Vailati, Peano's former collaborator and mentor of the Italian pragmatists, Kant did not consider the extreme influence of other disciplines – primarily aesthetics – on theoretical knowledge. Much worse, he did not understand the importance of the genealogical study of disciplines, including psychology, while his studies on judgments and categories ultimately relied upon it. Vailati criticizes Kant because he does not take into account the importance of evolution. This would be unfair if the Italian philosopher was referring not so much to Darwin's philosophical doctrine as to the mere development of the sciences that Kant was talking about. Ironically Vailati underlines that when Kant was still writing his first *Critique*, which relied on Newtonian physics, the non-Euclidean geometries had already made his thoughts seem old. Vailati and his disciple Calderoni make this criticism, which echoes other pragmatists in pointing out the ahistorical and formal weakness of the Kantian "I," and also criticize introspection as a research method. Externalism, which was Peirce's and would become Ludwig Wittgenstein's method of research about mental processes, is strongly proposed here.[13] Similarly to James, Vailati reaches very radical conclusions, though expressed only by letter to Papini in which he quotes an article appeared in the *Figaro* according to which Kant has "devoted his genius to disprove theories that no one had ever supported and to defend theses that no one had ever doubted, and concludes by saying that the free spirits admire him for the doubts that were his starting point, and non-free spirits admire him for the dogmatism to which he arrived" (Vailati 1971, 398, my translation).

In *Il crepuscolo dei filosofi,* Papini devotes a chapter to Kant, polemically analyzing him as a man, a moralist, and a theorist of knowledge. The first aspect has little philosophical importance although it can be taken as an ironic picture of Kant's rationalism; we can put it aside, observing the irony that Kant taught geography and yet "had never gone outside Könisberg for more than ten miles" (Papini 1906, 5). With regard to morality, Papini criticizes Kant for the form of his categorical imperative and for the postulate of freedom. According to Papini, in both cases, Kant derives his ideas from the feeling of universality and religious responsibility, because they cannot come from rational analysis. The alleged criticism results in an uncritical acceptance of certain feelings at the expense of others.

In the same way, Kantian theorizing requires an unknowable and inexplicable a priori. This a priori is unknowable because if a priori knowledge is part of knowledge, how would we know it analytically, separating it from what it is always conjoined? (ibid., 26–7). The a priori is inexplicable because even if we admitted to knowing it, we would not comprehend how it emerged into our knowledge since "Kant did not want to do psychogenesis and not even psychology" (ibid., 27). The same strategy applies to the noumenon: how can Kant mention what should not even be knowable? And if he knows it, how did this knowledge occur?

The criticism of the link between necessity and a priori is more interesting and innovative. Are analytic judgments really necessary? Papini distinguishes between two meanings of the term "necessary." If "necessary" meant "what cannot be otherwise," then everything that has already happened would be necessary but not a priori (ibid., 36). And if "necessary" meant "what cannot be said the opposite of without absurdity" – for example mathematics – then we would have only one type of bond due to the conventionality of definitions: the definition implies the concept that, if amended, would only fall beyond it. It is a nominal problem, which the analytic-synthetic distinction cannot justify. What is analytic was initially synthetic, and today's definitions are always subject to new synthetic evolutions over time.

The intellectualism of the a priori is also the central point of F.C.S. Schiller's critique of Kant. In "Axioms as Postulates" (1902) Schiller charges Kant's view in the first *Critique* as covertly psychological. According to the German-British thinker, Kant's a priori does not respect the way in which we experience reality. The construction of those a priori is a way to disguise Platonic dualism of form and matter. Schiller does not criticize the postulation of those a priori truths as a clever way to see experience, but despises the idea of removing their psychological nature, or of viewing them as anything other than aesthetical devices. If they were considered only axioms that need a postulation, Schiller would not oppose them. In this case we should study their history and their psychogenetics (1902, 431). This move is the one that Kant applies to practical reason and that Schiller would have liked him to apply to theoretical knowledge also. On the contrary, intellectualism hinders Kant from considering "the fact that the living organism acts as a whole" (ibid., 434). In the way in which Kant states them, "the most intelligent reader cannot but feel that the dualism of the Pure and Practical Reason is intolerable and their antagonism irreconcilable," while the dual character which is doctrine imposes "upon Kant as both the Cerberus and Herakles of the Noumenal world is calculated to bring ridicule both upon him and upon his system" (ibid., 436).

Therefore, pragmatists have collectively expressed this basic idea about Kant: he separates reality from knowledge, making "the thing-in-itself" unknowable (although often confusing the transcendental object and the thing-in-itself) and entrusting to the "I think" the task to reconstitute the lost unity. As we have seen in this short overview, there are many variations and specific branches of this thought, but it is integral to the viewpoint of American and European Pragmatists.

What do classic pragmatists oppose in this point of view? The answer runs through many threads according to different authors. However, I will sum it up according to three main topics that will be the philosophical background of my proposal: sign, continuity, and common sense. I will rely heavily on Peirce's account of them because it is more precise and more useful to my proposal, even though I find all pragmatists committed to them. At the end I will single out synthetic reasoning as the kind of research method that will continue to develop these topics in a pragmatist way.

## 2. SIGN

The concept of sign is the first landmark of Peirce's philosophy. I find this concept to be one of the most striking pragmatist legacies, even though it belongs mainly to Peirce. Peirce's representationalism is also the reason why Rorty excludes him from the pragmatist landscape. However, in the scientific research on signs Peirce overtakes Kant's epistemology – even though this theoretical shift emerged only in his later work. A new pragmatist proposal has to use this sophisticated tool, which also allows the freedom of interpretation for which Rorty advocates.

From the beginning, Peirce's semiotics was intended to deny the division between phenomenon and noumenon. Early writings show that Peirce wanted to abolish the idea of the unknowable from the start (*W1*, 37–44). Sure enough, the denial of his early philosophical steps has an Enlightened tone. It seems to go toward subjectivist idealism, while in his later years the same denial becomes the base of a scholastic realism of the Scotistic stripe – as Peirce was defining it referring to the theory of universals of medieval philosopher Duns Scotus (ca. 1266–1308) – or a sort of objective idealism.[14] In any case, from the start Peirce's semiotic does not follow Kant's representationalism. Peirce introduced a new form of representation centred on the analysis of the relationship between the representamen (namely, the sign itself), the object of reference, and the interpretant (namely, the function of interpretation).

The triad icon-index-symbol is justifiably one of Peirce's most renowned achievements. This triadic division grasps the fundamental relationships that arise between object and sign. Icons are signs that represent their object by similarity. Indices are signs that represent their object by direct contiguity or brute force. Symbols are signs that represent their object by interpretation. Through his use of signs, Peirce reaches the continuity that Kant's view was missing. There is no gap between reality and knowledge. We can question what the nature of reality is, but we cannot think that reality is somehow severed from knowledge. Far from being a legacy of the ancient idea of correspondence, Peirce's representationalism might even agree with some of the most advanced hermeneutical theories. The theory of signs can well fit a profound constructivism, as Margolis proposes.[15] Icons, indices, and symbols explain why our knowledge works and how it is indistinguishable from reality as such. Peirce himself will show this outcome in the celebrated series for the *Popular Science Monthly*: reality, knowledge, and a community of inquirers are one and the same thing, in the long run of inquiry (*EP1*, 136–41).

However, this integrated view is indeed as far away from constructivism as it is from Kantianism, and critics have long debated Peirce's ideas of reality and truth. They were puzzled by the contemporary presence of a strong hermeneutic side and of a strong realist vision. The enigma is grounded in the same structure of sign that Peirce proposed. The structure of signs is a triad composed of object / representamen / interpretant. The name "object" covers both the dynamic object – the object as it is in the flux of reality, the object that is never the same – and the immediate object – the common object of our representations (*EP2*, 495). In this careful distinction lies the core of Peirce's realism: in a sense our knowledge always stems from and arrives at the dynamic object, an *almost* incomprehensible object which is at the beginning of our knowledge and at the end of our complete representation. As long as this object is recognized, there is no room for a complete idealization of the pattern of knowledge.

On the other hand, interpretation is part of the sign itself because immediate, dynamical, and final interpretants are those signs that permit representamens to foster and finish their representative work. Interpretant is the seal that allows us to understand that sign has been received as and operated as a sign (De Tienne 2009). In the classification of signs in the letter to a Lady Welby of 4 October 1904 (*CP* 8.327–40), Peirce says that a sign in respect to an interpretant can be a rhema, a dicent or proposition, or an argument. Signs work when they are received at least as rhema; otherwise, they fail to be signs and remain at the level of pure clash between objects. Moreover, as scholarship has recognized unanimously, final interpretant coincides with a habit of action, so that the entire development of human experience and communication can fall under the heading of interpretations through signs (*EP2*, 412).[16]

It is no wonder that this double characteristic of hard objectivity and total interpretation baffled critics. However, the solution is that we cannot cast Peirce's – and the pragmatists' – view in a cage that is not theirs. Pragmatists are not idealists nor are they realists: they simply have a new concept of knowledge and experience, which can only be defined as "pragmatist." To understand that this is really a pragmatist view and not only Peirce's, consider this passage from William James's *The Meaning of Truth*:

> Investigation shows that, in the function called truth, previous realities are not the only independent variables. To a certain extent our ideas, being realities, are also independent variables, and, just as they follow other reality and fit it, so, in a measure, does other reality follow and fit them. When they add themselves to being, they partly re-determine the existent, so that reality as a whole appears incompletely definable unless ideas also are kept account of. (1911, 185–6)

Experience is thus made of ideas and facts, of ontology and epistemology. According to pragmatists, any view that would try to separate the two poles in any way is false. Vice versa, anything that links them is working as a mediator, namely as a sign.

> If I tell you how to get to the railroad station, don't I implicitly introduce you to the *what*, to the being and nature of that edifice? It is quite true that the abstract *word* "how" hasn't the same meaning as the abstract *word* "what," but in this universe of concrete facts you cannot keep hows and whats asunder. The reasons why I find it satisfactory to believe that any idea is true, the *how* of my arriving at that belief, may be among the very reasons why the idea *is* true in reality. (Ibid., 200–1)

## 3. CONTINUITY

"Pragmatist experience" has a conceptual root in the mathematical and philosophical notion of continuity. Peirce deepened the mathematical side of it, but all classic pragmatists used this model in their philosophy. Continuity was the way in which they translated Darwin's hypothesis on evolution into an epistemic and an ontological concept. On the epistemic level, consider James's stream of consciousness and substantive/transitive states of mind, Dewey's arc reflex model, and Mead's idea of symbolic gesture. On an ontological level, consider James' radical empiricism, Dewey's naturalized metaphysics of ends, and Mead's concept of temporality and the relationship between our central nervous system and the set of answers that compose meaning.

However, the more precise account of continuity comes from Peirce's mathematical studies. Peirce always recognized the importance of continuity, even in his early writings where he conceived of it as infinite divisibility (the Kantian view). Starting from the end of the 1880s, and thanks to his reading of Cantor, Peirce grasped a new way to reach this concept and, above all, its philosophical implications. These latter emerged in his series for the *Monist* (1892–93) (*EP1*, 285–371), as well as in his letters to William James in which he tried to present his course on logic, based on continuity (L224, 26 December 1893). Continuity is identified here with the ontological texture of experience and knowledge, according to the profound unity that defines the concept of pragmatist experience. In the *Monist* series, Peirce proposed the idea of synechism as the philosophical parallel of mathematical continuity: *synechism* implies *tychism* as the crucial theme of a continuity in which the *tyche*, namely chance, must be somehow comprehended. However, over the years, he deepened his mathematical studies on continuity, and in 1900 reached the proof of Cantor's theorem and paradox. Setting aside the discussions about what he really grasped of Cantor's ideas, or what he knew and did not know about Cantor's progress on his own doctrine (Moore 2007a), the philosophical result of those discoveries is worth noticing.

Peirce was profoundly unsatisfied with Cantor's idea of continuity as far as its philosophical implications were concerned. He called Cantor's continuity a "pseudo-continuity" (*CP* 6.176) and sought a different description of it. The problem was that for both semiotic and mathematical reasons, that kind of continuity remains a metrical representation of something that cannot but escape any metric measure. Peirce explained his point of view with the image of the blackboard and of the sand. If we draw a line on a blackboard, it is not the line to show what continuity is; rather, it interrupts a previous continuity, which was the one with the blackboard (ibid. 6.203–6). The continuity of the discontinuity of the line is understandable because of the continuity of the blackboard. No matter how hard we study the line, the real continuity precedes it. In the same way, no matter how much we analyze and separate the grains of sand, we could not build up the continuity of the beach by their sum (ibid. 6.168).

These examples show that continuity is something that lies beyond the grasp of our analytic power, and that it has to comprise of discontinuous elements. For the above-mentioned correspondence between epistemology and ontology, Peirce did not consider this result a problem. He simply thought that Cantor's paradox showed the "real" continuity *per absurdum* (Maddalena 2009, 137–92); accordingly, our knowledge by analysis cannot grasp the totality, leaving room for other kinds of reasoning. On the ontological side, Peirce never formulated a final definition of "real" continuity, but he strongly affirmed this metaphysical reality and built the entire structure of his late thought on it. He never succeeded, though, in providing a final version of continuity that respected its not-metrical nature and opened up the possibility of a transition between totality and singularity.

Peirce made some further steps in studying the logical modalities that should have explained this movement within a not-metrical continuity. Possibility, actuality, and necessity were well defined from a logical point of view, and they will furnish an important background for our next chapters. Except for this logical insight, continuity remained an unfinished study on both epistemic and ontological levels. However, the hypothesis of continuity was the real keystone of Peirce's pragmatism and, without mathematically adequate notions and with different interpretations, it can be argued that continuity was the keystone of the entire pragmatist movement. Also, their particular understanding of continuity molds the way in which pragmatists have interpreted time as "evolution." To pragmatists, evolution lost its Darwinian nominalist character that makes it emerge from variation and adaptation of individuals. Instead, evolution is a law that precedes individuals, and from this concept a completely different project arises: the point is not to understand how individuals can make evolution happen, but how evolution can be embodied in individuals. This reversal is the foundation of any reversal in any discipline that pragmatists tackled: from sociology to psychology, from mathematics to logic, and from metaphysics to physics, pragmatists have always thought that continuity was the explicative standpoint of their researches.[17]

## 4. COMMON SENSE

The third pragmatist achievement that I consider to be a permanent legacy of pragmatism in all its stripes is its respect for the logical validity of common sense. Pragmatists maintained that truth cannot be contrary to what common sense perceives: we can sometimes explain, account for, deepen the rich experience that we have described, but the "pragmatist experience" remains the test of any and every theory. All in all, it is what the pragmatic maxim was intended to be: a good criterion to avoid useless quarrels that violate common sense. Peirce explained this in his theological example of the opposition of transubstantiation vs. consubstantiation; essentially, it meant that some topics of discussion have little bearing on the everyday life of the common person, or on common sense reasoning in general (*EP1*, 131–2). Afterwards, he corrected the maxim, allowing for a more sensitive inclusion of possibility into the realm of reality. As he stated it in "A Sketch of Logical Critics" (1911): "The other fault of that essay ... [is] the generalization that there is no reality in any habit, or lasting state in which something would happen in case a certain condition should be fulfilled, unless that condition sometime actually is fulfilled, instead of reading in the phenomenon of mechanical equilibrium the lesson that a true "would be" is as real as an actuality" (*EP2*, 456). The same example of transubstantiation versus consubstantiation changed when Peirce thought about it again in 1902:

> The Roman church requires the faithful to believe that the elements of the eucharist are really transformed into flesh and blood, although all their "sensible accidents," that is, all that could be expected from physical experience, remain those of bread and wine. The Protestant episcopal church requires its ministers to teach that the elements remain really bread and wine, although they have miraculous spiritual effects different from those of ordinary bread and wine ... But the layman declares that he cannot understand the difference. "That is not necessary," says the priest, "you can believe it implicitly." What does that mean? It means that the layman is to trust that if he could understand the matter and know the truth, he would find that the priest was right. (*CP* 5.541)

However, this ampliative correction is only to increase the correspondence between our common-sensical experience and the logical awareness of it.

In general, pragmatists held to a critical approval of common sense. Since "pragmatist experience" is the alpha and the omega of knowledge, anyone who really wants to know has to consider and respect the common representation with which experience presents itself. This does not mean that first appearance is right, but it does mean that any further explanation has to account also for that first appearance. Common sense "evidence" and "questions" are fundamental tests of any inquiry, and pragmatists never lost this connection, neither in the tone nor in the content of their writings.

In Peirce the general pragmatist respect for common sense finds a logical justification. He explains that common sense is grounded in "vagueness," logically defined as a state in which the object is indeterminate and would require a further determination by the utterer (*EP2*, 351). In vagueness the principle of contradiction does not hold.[18] "Vague" is thus defined as opposed to something that is determinate and therefore "actual," and to something that is "general" – that is, something that requires further determination by the interpretant. Therefore, "vague," "actual," and "general" are points of transition of our knowledge and of its interpretation in propositions. Knowledge is a process of determination so that Peirce even imagined a state of "nascent" ideas, the state in which ideas are passing from vagueness to generality. Being the logical state of possibilities, vagueness is the richest ground for ideas. Some of the more important ideas live in this state: commonsensical belief in God, for example, trust in the absolute value of life, and rejection of incest. We cannot exactly determine why we have adopted these ideas, but we hold them with that "rational instinct" that is the deep root of our rationality.

We appeal to the same vagueness when we are formulating hypotheses and when we are creating something new. We look for possibilities, and we hold on to them because they are logically plausible – even if they still remain vague. In this way, common sense obtains its logical vindication even though it does not exhaust questions and doubts.[19] However, here I am interested in bringing the double characteristic of "change in time" (evolution) and of evidence that common sense brings into the open. Maurice Merleau-Ponty used to say that philosophers are those who have, inseparably, a taste for evidence and a feeling for ambiguity (1988, 4). A pragmatist translation would say that philosophers are rational beings who respect common sense, namely, that have both the taste for evidence and sensitivity to vagueness.

The importance of vagueness and of the transit among vagueness, actuality, and generality as its correspondent on the logical-ontological level among possibility, actuality, necessity will be a fundamental issue of my pragmatist proposal of a philosophy of gesture in chapter 4. I will return to common sense as morality in chapter 8, but throughout the book I will maintain focus on the pragmatists' attention to, and Peirce's logical understanding of, common sense.

## 5. CONCLUSION AND BEGINNING

The three features that I identified – the use of signs, epistemic and ontologic continuity, and the defense of common sense – exhibit a vague picture of the pragmatist way to do philosophy. Sure enough, such a picture reveals that one cannot understand pragmatism if one's anti-Cartesianism is not supplemented by a profound anti-Kantianism. Moreover, such a picture shows a new, richer way to look at experience as a unity of theory and practice, and a profound realist view of knowledge open to metaphysics. The different ways in which classic pragmatists underlined and arranged these common elements signify different attempts to cope with the problems of epistemology. However, classic pragmatists' epistemologies have not been widely recognized as strong alternatives to mainstream philosophies. My point is that this is due to the fact that they did not fully exploit the insights provided by these three fundamental features. Therefore, they presented interesting tools and decisive, but vague, pictures of epistemology and ontology. We can say that the vagueness of these pictures also shows that classic pragmatism has not finished its work. This is why it is so interesting to try to complete it, and to verify whether it is a good solution for contemporary philosophical issues.

The philosophy of gesture that I present is an attempt to push pragmatist insight toward a closer unification of experience and methods of inquiry, toward a different definition of synthesis and analysis, and toward what I call a "complete synthetic pattern." In order to reach this pattern, I must explain Peirce's late drive toward a form of complete syntheticity. I consider this attempt incomplete but meaningful. Peirce strove to reach a complete picture of our reasoning, but could not get to it because he was stuck within the Kantian definition of synthetic and analytic. Paradoxically, pragmatists fought against this Kantian vision that they inherited, but they inevitably collapsed under the main division imposed by the German thinker. From this perspective, they really belong to the philosophical movements of the twentieth century that adhered to an image of knowledge and science built up by Kant. Any reaction, such as existentialism and hermeneutics, only paraded the power of the Kantian pattern that required either acceptance or radical refusal. The pragmatists' many tools in different fields – logic, psychology, epistemology, metaphysics – point in another direction. They suggest that it is possible to take Kant's project as a small part of a broader project, exactly as contemporary mathematics took Cantor's analyses and Hilbert's formalizations as a small part of a broader realm (Zalamea 2008, 2012).

In the next chapter we will see that Peirce himself was elaborating on a broader project through his existential graphs, and we will observe that we need a different pattern of syntheticity and analyticity in order to put Peirce's insight to work.

# 2

# Peirce's Incomplete Synthetic Turn

The first step of our research concerns the attitude of pragmatism toward the synthetic-analytic dichotomy. From the pragmatic maxim onward, pragmatists stressed the importance of a kind of reasoning that will synthetically broaden knowledge. In order to represent a real way of reasoning within this continuous path, classic pragmatists forged rational tools. Peirce's abduction and Dewey's logic of inquiry are perhaps the most important and most useful methods of reasoning that they developed. These tools show the pragmatists' attempt to work out a different rational paradigm that would respect the continuity of experience. They tried to avoid any abstract distinction or division, and they allowed for a more ampliative way of thinking. Their tools show that pragmatism is alien to both any form of static Platonic essentialism and to many attempts to reduce knowledge to analysis or verificationism.

However, their tools remain an analytic way to approach synthetic reasoning. They never realized that their research pointed toward a complete synthetic pattern, where synthesis is achieved through synthetic tools. In order to comprehend both this tendency to syntheticity and this "failure," it is important to follow Peirce's footsteps. In fact, he was the pragmatist who represented possibly the best exemplification of this bivalence.

## 1. PEIRCE'S ENIGMAS

Peirce's pragmatism hides many enigmas. One of the most provocative is that it introduces many new philosophical tools – suffice it to mention semiotic, abductive logic, a heuristic based on continuity, and scholastic realism – all essential components of a never realized broader philosophical project. As is well known, there are several existential reasons to explain its incompletion,[1] but a question remains unanswered: what was the project he referred to while striving to give "the proof of pragmatism," the unattained aim of his late years?[2]

The project is not the proof itself. Rather, it is the reason for which the proof could not attain a final form. The proof never satisfied Peirce because it was always a partial view of something broader. Peirce usually identified this as being "the truth of continuity" or "the truth of synechism" (*EP2*, 335), or else the method of justifying the "nature of Sequence" (*MS* 330, 57) – namely, the nature of pragmatism. In other words, Peirce was looking for that broader picture of reasoning that we anticipated in the previous chapter, so much so that the proof required a vast panoptic view necessarily covering different fields. In a letter to William James, he wrote that even if every single part of his work had been published, "the principal thing would remain unpublished; for this depends upon the way the parts are filled together, which is not the most obvious of things and would then wholly escape notice" (L224, 1 December 1902). This comment raises the question: what was the overall project?

It was in the "Illustrations of the Logic of Science" (1877–78) that Peirce first furnished his own version of the logic of inquiry, the core of which was the pragmatic maxim within the realistic procedure of science. Notwithstanding the clarity of the maxim, his logic of inquiry presented also several difficulties that Peirce tried to fix by digging deeper roots and extending the branches of his logic. This ultimately required the elaboration of an entire classification of sciences and the study of several interdisciplinary topics.[3] In three series of lectures Peirce gave from 1898 to 1903, he pinpointed one or the other of these interdisciplinary themes. There are several possible orders for these scattered parts of his philosophy, even though all of them have to somehow follow the Classification of Sciences that Peirce proposed at the turn of the century. An ordered list of topics could be the one proposed in "Prolegomena to an Apology for Pragmaticism": continuity, phaneroscopy, signs, existential graphs, different kinds of reasoning. In the drafts and the articles of the series written for *The Monist* (1905–06) he also stressed the role of normative sciences.[4] In that entire series and in the years that followed, he tried in vain to fully explain this or a similar order he had in mind.

These efforts were "in vain" because Peirce tended to lose his track while tilling the "virgin soil" (*CP* 1.128) of those many fields of research he himself discovered. And here a complementary question arises: why did he get lost? Part of the reason is that all of the aforementioned topics were products of his original insight, and Peirce was eager to explain them precisely. The mathematical definition of continuity stemmed from his thirty years of studying Cantor's set theory, and Peirce had independently discovered Cantor's theorem (the cardinality – multitude – of the set of all subsets of any set is strictly greater than the cardinality of the set) and Cantor's subsequent paradox (the set of all sets is at once larger and smaller than the set of its subsets). Peirce could not know that Cantor had discovered the same paradox and, in contrast to the German mathematician, he saw the immense philosophical import of this discovery.[5] But in his lectures, papers, and drafts he spent a lot of time explaining the mathematical basis of the theorem. After 1900, he went on with the paradox, saving little time and space for its philosophical impact. As a result, his articles and manuscripts often treat either the mathematical explanation alone or the philosophical consequence alone, and it is difficult to put the two together.

Peirce was perhaps more successful with his explanations in phaneroscopy, semiotics, and logic. In these three fields he succeeded in accounting for the importance and the impact of those discoveries on our philosophical understanding, especially if one reads them in the light of the too-often discredited Classification of Sciences. Nonetheless, Peirce failed to provide a definitive sketch of semiotic grammar (Short 2007, 178), a thorough account of abduction – he was working to the end of his days on the relationship between abduction and "rational instinct" – and the actual description of the way in which we carry out a phaneroscopic analysis (De Tienne 2004, 15–29). Last but not least, when in the 1903 Lowell Lectures Peirce explained his existential graphs he left rather implicit how they were part of the answer to the question "what makes a reasoning sound?"

Again, all of these topics were brand new fields of inquiry, and Peirce had to spend most of his time convincing his reader or audience (or himself) that these fields existed and were worth studying. Of course, scholars tried to systematize all of them, but as much as we would like to believe that we have perfectly interpreted Peirce's thought on this or that topic, many of our reconstructions rely on our reading of Peirce's many – sometimes apparently inconsistent – manuscripts, namely on his attempts to clearly articulate what he meant, which were never definitive. He was the discoverer of so many new lands of thought that it would have been unfair to ask him to also be their explorer, organizer, and governor. What most deserves attention is Peirce's understanding that the real explanation of these new topics lay in the connection to one another and in the proof this connection affords for pragmatism, that is, for the sequence of thought.

## 2. KANT'S ANALYTIC HERITAGE

Another part of the reason for Peirce's failure in giving a final account of pragmatism is that he was looking for a completely new pattern of reasoning, even though he was not completely aware that he was doing so. Which was the completely different pattern? We can call it a "completely" synthetic pattern. What does that mean?

According to Kant, an analytic judgment subsumes a predicate under a subject, while a synthetic judgment has to look outside the subject-concept into experience, to capture how the predicate is connected to, but not subsumed within, the concept (*CRP* A7, B11).[6] Quine – and Saul Kripke after him – stressed that in Kant's work, the triad of analysis, aprioricity, and necessity form a circular cluster in which any element justifies, but also coincides with, the others. Analytic judgments are necessary because they are a priori, and being a priori they are necessary and hence analytic. In this way logic (analysis), epistemic (a priori), and metaphysical (necessary) levels coincide, furnishing the pattern of true or warranted knowledge.[7]

But Kant's aim was not at all the defense of the uniqueness of analytic judgments. He was aware that, as much as analytic judgments are important, they do not bring about the acquisition of new knowledge. They are really needed "only for attaining that distinctness in concepts which is required for a secure and extensive synthesis that, as such, will actually be a new acquisition" (*CPR* A10, B14). What is the kind of synthesis Kant was looking for?

There is a synthesis that is only the reverse of analysis. This is the operation of combining elements that come from the "dissection of concepts" produced by analysis. Once we have broken up the concept of the subject, we can list and work on the elements we find. As for the synthetic a priori judgments, they are supposedly different from any analysis and thus really manifest a "synthetic pattern." However, we will see that this difference turns out to be more virtual than real.

Here I will define synthesis according to the characteristics pointed out by Robert Hanna in his studies about Kant. I find Hanna's account trustworthy and fair to Kant's intention. That is why its results are so striking for the direction I want to take. Now, the characteristics of synthesis Hanna points out are as follows: 1) a judgment is synthetic when it "advances beyond the intension of that concept and establishes a novel connection with another concept"; 2) this connection is made possible by something "altogether different" from a conceptual content; 3) negation does not have to be a logical contradiction necessarily; 4) synthetic judgments amplify the intensional structure, whereas comprehension is narrowed (2001, 191).

Hanna points out that the first characteristic alone, the one Kant recognized as early as 1764, is not sufficient to guarantee an epistemic difference between analytic and synthetic. In the framework of the first *Critique*, the novel connection stated as first characteristic falls under the "original synthetic unity of apperception" as a combinatory synthesis of concepts. Hanna concludes correctly: "So, if one were then to consider the new complex concept generated by the novel conceptual connection as itself a given concept, then although a proposition was by hypothesis synthetic, the conceptual connection making up its content would paradoxically come out analytic" (2001, 191–2). This paradox threatens the whole project at every step: if synthesis is not completely independent from a conceptual framework, sooner or later during the process of knowledge, analyticity will take over. Every synthesis would turn out to be an analysis. That is possibly why Kant adds the three other characteristics that hint toward a completely independent, not-conceptual feature within our synthetic reasoning and judgment. This element is "intuition."

In order to respond to its decisive task, "intuition" must be defined as well. According to Hanna's reconstruction, intuition is immediate, related to sensibility, prior to thought, concerning singulars, and dependent on objects. These five characteristics show a strongly realistic account of syntheticity: a reasoning can be synthetic if it is determined by intuition, and intuition displays features that are not reducible to concepts in any way. Particularly striking and important for the rest of the book, syntheticity must rely upon an intuition of a singular object, avoiding any possible reduction of singularity of intuition to singularity of reference.

However, this strongly realist approach raises one question: What kind of necessity can we find in synthetic judgment built on intuition? Analytic judgments are necessary by virtue of the principle of contradiction, or in Kant's view, because predicates are contained within the subject (*CPR* B190–3) as a part in a whole. As problematic as this "containment" metaphor can be and as imprecise as his notions of logic were, Kant wanted to signify that analytic judgments are dependent on concepts and are independent from experience. Decomposition of the subject, or of the whole concept, or of the pattern of knowledge itself, cannot increase the intension of our knowledge even though it renders what we know to be more precise.

Synthetic judgments increase intension, but the price in terms of necessity and universality is high. Kant recalls that Hume despaired to find any necessity in these judgments, while Locke, who was drawing them from experience, lost consistency and hence necessity (*CPR* B128). In order to keep both necessity and syntheticity, Kant builds up the complicated path of the *Critique*, specifically the paradoxical unity of intuition and concepts. What kind of necessity does this union have? Can we really say that it is the same necessity that analytic judgment has?

Here a previous note returns. The project risked collapse if syntheticity relied only upon synthetic, original apperception. In that case, each piece of knowledge would turn out to be part of a given concept, and synthesis would turn into analysis. In this hypothesis the scheme "part-whole" would lead the inference again. Something is necessary because it is part of a whole. The relationship is granted by the scheme from the beginning. This approach would save necessity, but would lose the autonomy of the synthetic pattern of reasoning.

Hanna gives a more sophisticated account that fits Kant's insight better. In order to avoid the collapse of syntheticity into analyticity, Hanna distinguishes two kinds of necessity: "universal necessity" for analytic judgments and "restricted necessity" for synthetic judgments. In both cases the world is the truth-maker: in the first case a proposition is true only if it is true in every possible world, while in the second case a proposition is true only if it is true in an "experienceable" world, namely in a world accessible to intuition as it is described by the same *Critique* (2001, 239).

So stated, Hanna's account of Kant's syntheticity responds to our common sense experience and avoids previous collapse of syntheticity upon analyticity. However, a closer look at this foundation on the "restricted necessity" reveals that it did not really get rid of the threat, which is hidden at a deeper level.

We have seen that even if in a restricted form, synthetic judgments can bear necessity; we have also seen that intuition is the key element of synthesis. Now, we know that intuition is always bound to space and time, according to the model that Kant proposes in his transcendental aesthetics. When Kant speaks of a priori pure intuition of space and time, in particular when he finds a basis of aesthetics on intuition, he has to stress the importance of the singularity and totality of those intuitions. There is one space and one time. This uniqueness permits necessity that Hanna's interpretation describes well.

> Kant's claim is that space is represented by the representation of space as not only an individual, but as an individual whole composed of parts: "if one speaks of many spaces, one understands by that only parts of one and the same unique space." This whole, moreover, contains its spatial parts in a very special way, for "space is represented as an infinite *given* magnitude" (CPR A25/B39). Space, in other words, is represented as an infinite totality of spaces, such that every particular space is *already* contained within the one comprehensive space. But it is not as though space were a sort of massive chessboard with all individual spaces predetermined as occupants of tidy rows and columns; rather, the manifold of spaces is represented as resulting essentially from various limitations of the total space. This implies that even a collection of the individual parts of space as large as the complete set of natural numbers could not exhaust space, since counting the parts of space would be only one possible way of limiting it. Space is represented as a singular abstract totality that is logically irreducible and logically prior to any aggregate of particular subspaces or spatial items that it encompasses: "these parts cannot as it were precede the one all-embracing space, as its constituents (from which its composition would be possible), but rather are thought only *in it*." (2001, 224)

Kant cannot abandon uniqueness of space and time because this is an essential characteristic of every intuition. Synthetic truths need it in order to account for their certainty. If space and time were not unique, we could not necessarily draw that portion of them which corresponds, for example, to our geometrical truths (CPR B39). So, here we understand why the mechanism works. Uniqueness of space and time recreates with singular intuitions the scheme part-whole so that a not conceptual but intuitional decomposition is implicit in synthetic a priori judgment. Could we say that the "containment" metaphor that holds for analytic judgments relying upon concepts seems to apply also to intuitions? Kant obtains synthetic necessity by accepting that all intuitions are contained in the intuitions of one space and one time. In other words, Kant preserves necessity within the same part-whole scheme that is at work in analytic judgments. Even if we accept Hanna's account, universal and restricted necessity in this experienceable world are identical as far as their structures are concerned. In both, necessity relies upon a relationship between part and whole.

This is the reason why even when Kant talks about the original synthetic unity of apperception as the kind of combination that analysis presupposes, he qualifies it as "pure," not empirical, "one and the same" (*CPR*, B 132). The unity that this pure apperception creates is "transcendental" (ibid.), and "precedes a priori all my determinate thought" (ibid. 177, B 135). Synthesis precedes analysis, but the character of universality (here conjoined with "sameness") and aprioricity would shape it according to the analytic pattern. This pattern remains the ideal example of all knowledge.

The consequences show the ambiguity of the origin. Following his analysis of the categories, Kant's solution to the synthetic working of judgment is the transcendental schematism that is wholly a fruit of the aprioricity (and thus necessity, and thus analyticity) of categories[8] through a "reproductive imagination" that is again "pure" and "a priori" (ibid. 224; A 142, B 181). The schema works according to "a rule, expressed by the category, of unity according to concepts as such" (ibid.). "The presentations of objects must cohere a priori ... in one concept" (ibid.). As Peirce himself noticed, a schema is still "general as a concept" (*CP* 5.531). Peirce meant his comment to be positive, but it shows that Kant's schematism falls short of what should have been the concrete understanding of categories.

Summing up, the idea of knowledge is really founded upon an analytic pattern, and that is why Kant seeks to solve the problem of knowledge by using critical – that is, analytic – tools only. Kant provides an analysis of synthetic judgments whereby he defines[9] (analytically) the steps through which we arrive at a synthetic representation of reality. Only by breaking down this path step-by-step would Kant be sure to grasp the substance of what knowledge is. The only real synthesis would come up with the *Critique of Judgment*, but once again it will have a form that combines (adds to one another) elements of the two previous critiques.

In this way Kant simply systematized the long heritage of Western philosophy, but he made clear that theoretical or pure knowledge is either analytic or something that is analyzable, namely broken down into necessary, a priori pieces of a whole.

## 3. PEIRCE'S WAVERING AND PRAGMATISTS' STRIVING FOR SYNTHETICITY

Young Peirce showed no awareness of the complex, presupposed circularity among aprioricity, analyticity, and necessity.[10] But he had enough philosophical insight to sense immediately that something was missing. As early as 1869, in "Validity of the Laws of Logic," he pointed out that far more fundamental than the possibility of synthetic a priori reasoning was the possibility of merely synthetic judgments (*W2*, 267–8).[11] Peirce wanted to go further than Kant in criticizing judgments, and to do so he discarded the a priori principle. A different path of reasoning was needed, and Peirce tried to provide it through both semiotics and the a posteriori method of science. Accordingly, Peirce listed aprioricity as one of the weak, ineffective methods for fixing a belief (*W3*, 252–3). The method of science always remained for Peirce an a posteriori method; he spent his life trying to explain and justify the nature of "ampliative" reasoning, another phrase for synthetic reasoning.

However, when in the 1877–78 *Popular Science Monthly* series Peirce gave the justification for induction – which at the time he thought included also hypotheses – he surprisingly relied metaphorically on an "extension" of the a priori principle. It is of course a rhetorical expedient, since Peirce's conception of experience had already been forged in the semiotic a posteriori hearth, but it is still a significant episode.

> It will be interesting to see how the answer which Kant gave to his question about synthetical judgments a priori will appear if extended to the question of synthetical judgments

> in general. That answer is, that synthetical judgments a priori are possible because whatever is universally true is involved in the conditions of experience. Let us apply this to a general synthetical reasoning. I take from a bag a handful of beans; they are all purple, and I infer that all the beans in the bag are purple. How can I do that? Why, upon the principle that whatever is universally true of my experience (which is here the appearance of these different beans) is involved in the condition of experience. The condition of this special experience is that all these beans were taken from that bag. According to Kant's principle, then, whatever is found true of all the beans drawn from the bag must find its explanation in some peculiarity of the content of the bag. This is a satisfactory statement of the principle of induction. (*W3*, 304)

Peirce would then explain that synthetic inference is founded upon a classification of facts, not according to their characters, but according to the manner of obtaining them, thus ensuring only the "degree of trustworthiness of our proceeding" (ibid., 305). In this way Peirce transforms Kant's a priori principle into a methodological guarantee resting on a certain interpretation of the general statement that "whatever is universally true is involved in the conditions of experience." So then the idea of necessary, universal truth moves from Kant's a priori categories into Peirce's methodological conditions. In such a passage universal, a priori truth loses part of its "necessity" by becoming merely "trustworthy." Still, the path Peirce follows remains through the idea of necessity or universality. Like Kant with his schematism, Peirce is pursuing synthetic reasoning – but he gets to it through the analytic path. The outcome is that ampliative or synthetic arguments do not tend to the necessity of content but to the necessity of method.[12]

As we have seen, Peirce's attitude toward Kant was ambivalent. On the one hand he always remained somehow the admirer of Kant that he was in his youth; on the other hand, in his later years he presented strong critical statements and he assumed anti-Kantian positions.[13] Not surprisingly, while preparing the Lowell Lectures of 1903, Peirce's conscious and declared purpose was to give a complete analysis of our thinking.[14] "Synthetic," in Peirce's later years, has two kinds of meaning. One meaning is implied in the expression "synthetic philosophy," the kind of knowledge that "embraces all that truth which is derivable by collating the results of the different special sciences" (*EP2*, 372). This meaning corresponds to the inversion of the analytic decomposition. The other meaning is the one we find in the third Lowell Lecture where Peirce distinguishes synthetic from analytic judgments, attributing the former to mathematics (hence to necessary reasoning) and the latter to logic, which tries "to find out how necessary and probable inferences are composed" (*MS* 458, 4). Once again, logic is confined to the analytic scheme of composition/decomposition. Therefore, reasoning can be necessary or ampliative, but the logician's work is in both cases to find its composition, confirming that analysis presides over our methodological research even when, as in induction or hypotheses, it does not preside over the concepts at stake. Curiously, this opposition between mathematical/synthetic and logical/analytic methods goes back to Kant himself, even if it was completely understood within the Kantian frame of knowledge.

> Philosophical cognition, accordingly, regards the particular only in the general; mathematical the general in the particular, nay, in the individual. This is done, however, entirely a priori and by means of pure reason, so that, as this individual figure is determined under certain universal conditions of construction, the object of the conception, to which this figure corresponds as its schema, must be cogitated as universally determined. (*CPR* A711, B739)

Now, this distinction will become significant to my project because I will try to supplement Peirce's analytic project with the synthesis that mathematics already displays: a kind of synthesis in which universals are known in the particulars. I find this intention as the not-aware background of Peirce's and pragmatists' attempts to renovate epistemology.

As a matter of fact, in spite of Peirce's analytic project pragmatism chiefly concerns our concrete, synthetic way of thinking. The synthetic process, however, is not the Kantian one that seeks to attain, in both form and content, the kind of clearness that analysis has. All the tools Peirce crafted – from the list of categories to perceptual judgments, from the pragmatic maxim to abduction, from existential graphs to rational instinct – describe a changing synthetic process of thinking rather than the fixed analytic/synthetic reasoning (and judgment) described by Kant. This tension between the analytic background of his thought and the "completely synthetic" purpose of those same analyses also explains Peirce's progressive shift from Kant to Hegel, and his more and more evident epistemic turn in the philosophy of science.[15]

Even more generally, in the whole of pragmatism a love of synthesis itself in the concrete development of scientific reasoning prevails, a development which is well-represented by the degree of clarity that Peirce ascribes to ideas: familiarity, definition, pragmatic maxim, concrete reasonableness.[16] One can find the same attitude in James's attention to the relationship between psychology and epistemology, Dewey's logic of inquiry, and Mead's concept of significant symbol. Pragmatism was and is strongly committed to both understand and use ampliative, namely "synthetic," reasoning and to grasp its concrete way of acting. The extreme case of this synthetic striving is the consideration of tools and experiments as part of our logic, which leans toward what I call a "complete synthetic" pattern of reasoning or a "synthetic" philosophy.

The tension among an aspiration to a complete syntheticity as a supplement to analyticity, some very synthetic tools, and a not completely realized synthetic turn are thus the characteristics of the entire movement of thought. This tension makes us see a different kind of possibility. How could we define "synthetic" and "analytic" starting from the elements of sign and continuity that we considered linchpins of pragmatism in the previous chapter?

# 3

# A New Paradigm for Reasoning

## 1. THE PROPOSAL OF A NEW PARADIGM

In this chapter I propose new definitions for synthetic, analytic, and vague judgments. These definitions are sensitive to the central role that continuity and change play in Peirce's and the pragmatists' philosophy. It is important to notice that this proposal is no longer a philological research on pragmatists. Rather, it is a way to foster and supplement the classical pragmatists' conceptions of analyticity and syntheticity, a way to complete their incomplete revolution.

I will try to explore this redefined kind of synthetic judgment using some of the tools Peirce already analyzed. Mainly the tools I will use are those he mentioned when working on continuity and existential graphs. Of course, this part can also be taken as a semiotic study on Peirce's existential graphs, but it is worth recalling that this is not its main aim. In the next chapter I will propose the tool that fits this different synthetic pattern, and it will be clear that the historical section is definitely over.

The new definitions are as follows:

- A synthetic judgment (and reasoning) is a judgment (and reasoning) that recognizes identity through changes.
- An analytic judgment (and reasoning) is a judgment (and reasoning) that loses identity through changes.
- A vague judgment (and reasoning) is a judgment (and reasoning) that it is blind to identity through changes.

Two questions arise immediately while I am formulating this new set of definitions: a) why do we need a new definition? and b) why *this* new definition?

a) One of the reasons for this change is required by Peirce's and the pragmatists' failed attempt to give an overall, definitive picture for the many tools they provided. As I hope to show, their tools and results hinted at a more radical shift of paradigm in which all those scattered elements fit.

Beyond that, there are other compelling reasons for the proposed change of pattern. One is the clear impasse of analytic philosophy. That kind of philosophy, to which contemporary thought owes so much for its precision and productivity, seems now stuck in scholasticism, full of definitions detached from experiential reality and not really committed to improving our understanding of the world and its transformations. The fact is that analytic philosophy has now come to manifest the incompleteness of the criterion of necessity-analyticity-a prioricity displayed by Kant. And its critics, most importantly Quine and Kripke, offered only internal criticisms that failed to change the criterion itself.[1]

The good results of analytic philosophy are due to an efficient understanding of a certain kind of logic (symbolic logic) based on a certain kind of mathematics (set theory). But the "scholasticism" currently in vogue underlines a limitation of that logic: though analytic logic serves well to split up definitions, it is intrinsically a never-ending process. From science to grammar, definitions rarely provide an exact fit: they are always too loose or too tight. A definition is a useful tool but not the only one, and certainly not one capable of grasping changes in reality. New mathematics and new kinds of logics have already arisen: the time has come to try a new philosophical paradigm.[2] This study does not want to deny, minimize, or deconstruct the success of analytic reasoning as it has been carried out so far. I only want to show that analytic reasoning needs, and has always used, a complementary type of understanding in order to work properly. The possibility of both and the transition between them are the pillars of this different view. We will see that the logical core of synthetic reasoning is both analytically and synthetically describable. Arising from Peirce's studies, this view immediately understands the logical importance of vagueness, as the indispensable complement to the two proposed kinds.

A pragmatist account of syntheticity can be useful at this point.[3] Pragmatism has represented a third way in the twentieth-century philosophical landscape, between continental and analytic philosophies. Pragmatism can provide an alternative without losing the efforts and the results of other philosophical traditions of the last century. Pragmatism shares the love of precision with analytic philosophy – so much so that it was often mistaken for a peculiar version of neo-positivism. On the other hand pragmatism shares, with the most advanced hermeneutics, the pivotal role of interpretation in the configuration of meaning and the profound appraisal of reconfiguration, re-interpretation, and re-construction. The change of paradigm allows for a more comprehensive acceptance of all these aspects at the same time. This perspective justifies the fact that many authors talked about a pragmatic turn in contemporary philosophy. The turn was not really toward pragmatism, but toward a different broader picture of reasoning. Pragmatism was preparing the way for it more than any other twentieth-century philosophies.

b) The second question asked why *this* new definition. Synthetic reasoning is the original kind of reasoning that we use in everyday life, and it needs a new paradigm. I will try to explain and justify the new paradigm in the following sections.

Syntheticity will be understood and demonstrated according to the fundamental hypothesis of continuity. Before going into the technique of the demonstration, I want to begin with the core of the idea. Syntheticity as illustrated by Kant in the *Critique of Pure Reason* is a static limited aspect of a more general nature, which the above-mentioned formula can explicate. Roughly, it says that any synthetic judgment is really an action that establishes an identity between different aspects of experience. Even for Kant 7+5=12 was a sort of judgment that required "experience." What Kant did not realize was that the operation of fingers or stones that he had to imagine in order to explain syntheticity (*CPR*, B15–16) is not only an example but the nature of syntheticity itself. Any synthetic judgment coincides with the operation we have to perform in order to get at it. Kant calls synthesis the transcendental path of this operation, which is only a limited and highly questionable aspect of the entire action. Using the hypothesis of continuity and the richness of "pragmatist experience" we will define this action as continuity within a continuity. Nature, structure, and the limits of this continuity will be the subjects of the next point.

The second aspect that may be derived from the formula of this new paradigm is that synthesis coincides with "recognizing an identity": the action of establishing an identity between two "objects" is the judgment itself. Which is this "action"? And what are these objects? These are the questions that I have to clarify. Let us start with the "objects." The pragmatist view of experience does not distinguish between subject and object because it focuses on the relations among parts or portions of a changing reality. William James held that there are substantive and transitive moments of thought and reality.[4] Our judgments are the substantive part: the new paradigm helps to understand that these moments are parts of a broader transitional movement. In other words, our transitional experience stops at a certain provisional point of which the proposition is an expression. What we are really doing in this moment is completing a segment of our experience that establishes an identity between that provisionally final point and the initial, vague experience that we want to determine.

The new formula of kinds of judgments advocates a view in which the static judgment "this body is heavy" is part of the transition and of the operation that make us maintain the judgment itself. As we will see, in this operation we are always transforming a vague experience of an object (as a web of relations) into a singular experience. This experience is one that determines those aspects about which we are inquiring, and that can be generalized in a habit of action. "This body is heavy" is the recognition of a certain aspect that we were vaguely experiencing and about which we were inquiring. The identity is between the initial vague experience of the body and the determinate experience that can be generalized in the proposition. The process that leads to the proposition links the initial vague experience to the generalized one of the proposition through a singular action with that determinate part of experience that we call "body." The identity is always between two experiences of the same relationship(s). Occasionally, the second experience can be formulated by a proposition, but a proposition is only one of its possible realizations that can be more or less complete as any other synthetic action.

The second problem is about "action." Is any action synthetic? No, it is not, as experience shows. Or rather, there are several degrees of synthesis and very different kinds of actions. The point of my proposal is to identify the elements of synthetic action, to provide some good illustrations of it, to discern the different kinds of action, and to reveal the degrees of synthesis that they allow. This task will be the topic of the next chapter.

According to the picture that I present, three celebrated pragmatist affirmations make new and brighter sense. The first one is the fact that research is always tied to problem solving. Dewey was the pragmatist who most insisted on this point, and in this paradigm his concern finds an answer internal to logic. The problem we have to solve is always the vagueness of the experience that we want to determine. The second affirmation is about belief as "the demi-cadence which closes a musical phrase in the symphony of our intellectual life" (*EP1*, 129). Peirce was arguing that we make inquiries in order to reach the core of a belief, and that a belief is self-conscious, satisfactory, and habitual (namely, it involves the establishment of a habit of action). We will see that the new paradigm better fits Peirce's urging of pragmatism toward a complete intertwining of theoretical reasoning and practical action according to a purpose ("pragmatisch"). Third, the "game" between transitivity and substantivity explains the necessary affirmation of fallibilism. As experience happens, no proposition can be absolutely final.

This chapter will investigate how this general picture can be plausibly defended with the instruments that come from semiotics.[5] The reader who does not want to go into the technical Peirce-driven details of the definitions of the new paradigm can skip to the next chapter. Gestures will there be considered as the main tool of synthetic reasoning understood according to the new paradigm.

## 2. WHAT IS "CHANGE"? CONTINUITY

In order to show the plausibility of our paradigm, the first task is to explain "change" and how we can study it. The two questions go together if we use Peirce's fundamental insight: the concept of continuity, the "keystone" of pragmatism. To understand change in this sense, we need to use a mathematical and a logical approach.

### 2.1 *Mathematical Gestures*

From the very beginning of Peirce's intellectual proposal, continuity has played a central role. Continuity is already paired with representation – or cognition – in the 1868–69 *Journal of Speculative Philosophy* series (*EP1*, 11–82). Peirce never gave up this pairing, which became increasingly unified as he discovered the real mathematical structure of continuity.

There are many changes over time in Peirce's mathematical approach to the topic, but substantially they all focus on the proof of Cantor's theorem and paradox that Peirce independently discovered in the late 1890s. With this proof, Peirce understood that there is an infinite series of multitudes that Cantor's set theory can reach, but that those multitudes are always bounded to an imperfect or pseudo-continuity. This pseudo-continuity depends on the unavoidable singularity of the initial definition of a set or collection (*NEM3*, 774–5).[6] Peirce's definition of a set or collection implies that a collection is an individual whose existence depends on the regularities among other individuals. These "regularities" can be identified by the characteristics its members possess (in this case they are *ineunts*) or exclude (*exeunts*). To be singularly existent means to have one quality that defines the collection while the rest of the universe does not have that quality or does not have it in the same sense (*NEM3*, 776). Therefore, the definition of a collection leads immediately to the impossibility of grasping the "totality" by increasing multitudes. If a collection implies by definition *ineunts* and *exeunts* – namely a scheme of otherness – the collection of all the collections, not having by definition any exeunt, is unthinkable. Cantor's paradox mathematically confirms this evidence that Peirce first attains through the categorical status of individual. Therefore, the real continuity is beyond any calculation that set theory can reach.

So what is this "real" or "perfect" continuity, which is beyond the "pseudo-continuity" that sets can reach? Peirce changed his mind many times on this issue, initially trying to tie continuity to necessity and then to possibility.[7] Peirce first thought of making continuity the complete evolution of reality, the perfect "generality" in his logical terms. In this version (1900–05), any singularity is a rupture of perfect continuity, like a chalk mark on a blackboard. But afterwards (1907–14) he connected continuity to a more complex pattern in which continuity is a possibility, namely a model that may be realized. Singularities are now realizations of that original possibility tending to a general cohesiveness (*CP* 4.642; *MS* 204, 10–18).

It is in this second sense that our conception of change must be seen. We can understand change as a perfect continuity of possibilities of which any actual occurrence is a realization. In other words, whenever we reason about something existent, we are also reasoning about something that changes according to a possible model and following general conditions. Using Peirce's insight about continuity, we understand this change not as a property but as a reality to which our existent things belong. So if we want to explain this "belonging," we really have to refer to what continuity is. As we will see later, Peirce would add modalities to his explanation in order to specify what he meant. But for now, let us stick with Peirce's definition according to which continuity is a law (general) whose internal regularity is "an immediate connection" that we can understand as the condition of every possible realization (*CP* 4.642).

Of course change seems to imply "time," which Peirce himself points to as the model for this "immediate connection," and which Mead will use extensively (1932). However, I prefer to refer to "change" generally to avoid being entangled in a protracted discussion of the psychological and philosophical properties and consequences that "time" entails.

According to Zalamea, we can define a Peircean perfect continuum by four characters: modality (plasticity), transitivity, generality, and reflexivity. Each of these four characters underlies one aspect of the relationship between the parts and the whole of continuity.[8] I will take Zalamea's terms in their philosophical meaning. *Generality* is the law of cohesiveness among parts beyond any individual and any possibility of metrically measuring it; *modality* means plasticity, namely the fact that a continuum is not tied only to actualities but involves also possibility and necessity; *transitivity* is the internal passage between modalities (possibility, actuality, and general necessity); *reflexivity* means that any part shall have the same properties of the whole to which it belongs.

How should we study this "real or perfect" continuity? Peirce's official answer is: by existential graphs. I will make good use of this insight later on. In preparation for it, I want to underline a characteristic of Peirce's studies on mathematics that will be decisive for both the existential graphs and our logical paradigm.

The discovery of Cantor's paradox did not generate any doubt about the foundations of mathematics in Peirce (or in Cantor). How is that possible? The answer is that "perfect continuity" is real, and as such it guarantees our reasoning, even though the foundation that reality can provide will come a posteriori and not a priori.[9] But how could Peirce be so sure about it? It is part of the maxim of pragmatism – and indeed of our everyday synthetic reasoning – that "working" is the necessary and sufficient condition of reality. "If it works, it is." So, our "doing mathematics," our scribing graphs and diagrams, whether on the sheet of the mind or on some physical sheet, works: mathematics is one of the most developed and successful sciences. According to Peirce it is so because it imagines hypotheses and draws from them necessary conclusions. Therefore if we cannot doubt that it works, at the most we can wonder how it works.

Here we find the first hint of the syntheticity we are looking for. Mathematical diagrams work because they act synthetically, namely – according to the already mentioned Kantian definition that Peirce knew very well – in mathematics we are dealing with universals in particulars, while in philosophy we have to deal with universals abstracted from particulars (*CRP*, A711, B739).[10] The great power of generalization of mathematics is due to these contracted universals: our image of a triangle is good for any triangle and for any of its properties because in the particular triangle that we draw on the blackboard we are referencing what is universally understood to be a "triangle." Therefore, doing mathematics means already dealing with the reality of universals. There is no surprise that while we are doing mathematics we are constructing a broader metaphysical reality.

Setting aside the ontological issue, I will call "mathematical gesture" this synthetic approach to mathematics through our "doing mathematics."[11] We will have to find a parallel way of contracting universals in particulars and singulars in our everyday reasoning that moves within continuous change.

## 2.2 *Modalities*

There is a second interrelated approach to "change" in Peirce's late writings. It is the approach through logical modalities. Peirce's understanding of logical modalities grew during the years, reaching a more and more realistic view at the turn of the twentieth century. Possibility, actuality, and necessity became the way in which Peirce explained transition within the continuum itself. If Cantor's paradox showed the existence of an original higher continuum of reality that exceeds our computations, modalities define the internal life of this continuity. As we have already seen, Peirce's understanding of the modality of continuity swerved from necessity to possibility. He found a final version in which continuity is made of possibilities whose internal cohesiveness is necessary. But in what do these modalities consist?

Summing up Peirce's conception, possibility is the mode of reality in which the principle of contradiction does not hold: two alternative options can be true at the same time and according to the same aspect. Actuality or existence is the mode of reality in which both the principle of contradiction and the excluded third hold: in something actual or existent, when one of the two alternative options is true, the other is false, and no other option is available or thinkable. Peirce had trouble deciding whether actuality was a modality or coincided with an assertion "without modality" (*MS* 678, 47). He eventually maintained the former, as it added "a due sense of his responsibility" to the mere affirmation of a state of facts (ibid.). Necessity is the mode of reality in which the principle of the excluded third does not hold. That is to say that both alternatives can be false. In Peirce's mind, the possible negation of both alternatives implies that the necessity is something that we can affirm through a conditional future. Necessity is the state of things that "would be" true, if certain conditions happened. The conditional future involves the possible denial of two existent alternatives: "it is necessary that it will rain" or "it is necessary that it will not rain" can both be false because necessity states that "it would rain, if certain conditions of the weather happened."

All three modalities are discovered through assertion, and Peirce is perfectly aware that there is a difference between modalities *de dicto* and *de re*, and that the confusion between them is the source of human beings' gullibility. One can believe that something can really be ("real modality") because it may be ("ratiocinative modality") (ibid., 49). But acknowledging the difference between *de dicto* and *de re* does not mean denying the relationship between the logical and ontological realms: Peirce uses the denial of assertions in any modality (*de dicto*) to uncover their ontological status (*de re*).[12]

Peirce's short version of the three different modalities are expressed by three different phrases: there are the "may be's" (possibilities), "actualities," and "would be's" (necessities or generalities). Peirce claimed that all three modalities were real, meaning that they are independent from what any number of minds can think, or rather, that they coincide with the evolving continuity of reality. Reality actualizes possibilities and tries to develop them as generalities in an ongoing process of growing reasonableness (*EP2*, 255). (I will return to reasonableness later on.) According to Peirce, it is impossible to describe reality without modalities.

But one would expect the same internal life of the modalities to be replicated within our lower-level logic, in conformity with the reflexivity that is a property of Peirce's continuum. The logic of modalities implies a different understanding of stechiology (doctrine of elements). A term can be vague, determinate, and general (ibid., 350–3) according to the characters inhering in them both positively and negatively. If any character is predicated universally and affirmatively or recognized as inherent, the term is determinate. If it requires further determination by the utterer, it is vague; if it requires further determination by the interpretant, it is general. Vagueness, determination, and generality fall under the same description of the logical modalities, and they manifest the impact of logical modalities on the elements of our everyday assertions.

What we have here is a transition in determination that is based on the ontological reality of the logical modalities. A term or a concept can be vague and become determinate and even general, as I mentioned in section 1. Peirce also explains that there must be nascent states between indeterminate and determinate, and even between general and vague – that is, between the two indeterminacies (ibid., 353). In this way, he wants to protect the transition among categories in order to guarantee that logic be a fair representation of the continuity of reality.

In order to show how this transition occurs, I stress the importance Peirce ascribes to the first part of this trichotomy. Vagueness has such an importance because it is the possible state of things from which ideas stem. It is worth noticing that the whole explanation takes place in the article "Issues of Pragmaticism" (ibid., 346–59) in which Peirce elaborates on his critical common-sensism, pointing out that most of our beliefs and acritical inferences are initially and intrinsically vague. This vague starting point should not undermine their importance. On the contrary, their vagueness is a proof of their original springing from the continuum of reality. Belonging to the continuum of reality, they express the whole richness of reality at an incipient stage that is bound to become clearer as changes emerge. But "clearer" does not necessarily coincide with "richer." More often than not, powerful meanings for existence remain vague forever, and only a few of them acquire more advanced, logical determination. In logic, abductive hypotheses display the importance of the logical state of vagueness. Abductive inferences have often to rely upon characters that are vague, and they rarely come up with an already determinate hypothesis. They are the only way in which science can move forward, even though they are the most uncertain kind of inferences.[13] To add to this quick sketch, Peirce also pinpoints the relationship between the character of a term and the quantity of a proposition: particular corresponds to vague, singular to determinate, universal to general. Since ideas, inferences, and propositions have to imply a quantity, modalities have an impact at every level of logical structure.

Finally, according to Peirce's late attempts to weave together different parts of his philosophy (ibid., 496–9), we could add that modalities can also affect the method of apprehension of ideas as stated in the famous 1878 article "How to Make Our Ideas Clear." Peirce seems to match "vagueness" with familiarity (the first degree of clarity), "determination" with definition (the second degree), and generality with the pragmatic maxim (third degree). This last statement clarifies that the status of generality, universality, and pragmaticity is the highest one, the one through which our reasoning is proven to be sound. (The exception to this is concrete reasonableness itself,[14] which is a kind of super-generality capable of experiencing singulars within a general order) (ibid., 255). But this evidence would not come about without the entire undertaking of determination.

Let us now come to our definition of change. Our stance for realism allows this definition to hold both for "change" and "changing something": *a continuous reality in continuous transition among modalities.* Logical features respect Zalamea's four characteristics of the continuum: reflexivity, generality, modality, transitivity (plasticity). Every element has the same properties of general modalities (reflexivity); the passage among vagueness, determination, and generality (transitivity) is the law of the development of meaning through categories (generality); the latter depends on the possible inchoative status of vague meaning (modality).

How are we going to account for it in our reasoning? We said that synthetic reasoning is about "recognizing an identity through changes" and that the other kinds of reasoning derive their definition from this one. Now, knowing a little more about what a Peirce-derived conception of "change" is, we need to understand what we mean by "recognizing."

### 2.3 *Recognizing through Existential Graphs*

In the history of philosophy, there are at least two principal models for recognition. One provides for the permanence of certain attributes that allow us to identify an object, while the other refers somehow to the Hegelian dialectic, which then takes place in an idealistic or hermeneutic sphere.[15] Neither the recognition of attributes nor dialectical recognition seem to have the characteristics we need; we want to trace the logical pattern of recognizing and, at the same time, avoid the presuppositions of fixed attributes. We want to respect the movement of life and thought, but avoid the mechanism and the conceptualism that grounds Hegel's dialectic. It is another case of the application of the pragmatist "third way" to philosophical issues, a way that preserves both a precise method and an open interpretation.[16]

In order to understand what is going on in "recognizing an identity through change," in our "synthetic reasoning," the reasoning mostly used in everyday life and in many difficult cases of hypothetical reasoning (scientific discoveries, medical diagnoses, trials based on circumstantial evidences), or in our pragmatic understanding of meaning, we can rely on Peirce's study of the existential graphs (EG). The EG were the way in which Peirce himself sought to represent continuity, and are possibly one of the few scientific strategies for grasping the structure of "recognizing." As a matter of fact, EG are an alternative to symbolic logic: a "map of thought" not by symbolization, but by iconization.[17] In so far as they are iconic, they allow a closer relation to "objects."[18] As many authors have pointed out, EG are the iconic formalization of logic of propositions (alpha), first order (beta), and modalities (gamma). As we know, all of those logics were successfully formalized in a symbolic logic during almost the same years. However, EG show that an iconic level better guarantees the representation of the mathematical reality on which logic relies, allowing for the representation with the same tools of more complicated and open logical patterns (Zalamea 2010).

Sure enough EG were still analytic – but, as already stated, their overall (almost unconscious) project was a synthetic one.[19] Insofar as being a "map" (*CP* 4.513; *MS* 300, 52) or "a moving picture of thought" (*MS* 300, 23), capable of representing the creation of explanatory conjectures (ibid. 296, 8), EG tried to grant the traceability of "critical common sense" and its evidence. It is from the latter standpoint that we need to start in order to understand how EG can be used to explain what "recognizing" is.

## 3. EVIDENCE AND GENERALIZATION

According to Peirce, EG can show the path of any reasoning with evidence (Peirce started with the deductive one, but then he thought of expanding the field of applications of graphs to any kind of reasoning) (*CP* 4.530). Of course, at first reading, "evidence" does not sound like a very Peircean word. Peirce and pragmatists are often presented as skeptics or relativists as much as they are often introduced as pre-neo-positivists. On the contrary, pragmatism simply has its own form of certainty. The knowledge of the whole range of Peirce's research reveals that in his mature philosophy he was defending perception as a perception of generality (*EP2*, 222–4). So he thought that the diagram-icons enhanced by symbolic interpretation furnished by EG could make us perceive the generality according to which a conclusion follows from premises: "What is this 'Evidence'? It consists in the fact that the truth of the conclusion is *perceived*, in all its generality, and in the generality the how and why of the truth is perceived" (*NEM4*, 317). EG's project was to exhibit the changing path of our thought. With this first purpose, we already find the double characteristic of EG: analytic as explanation, but synthetic as project. Using the phrase introduced above, they are a kind of mathematical gesture and from this point of view they are synthetically conveying universals into singulars. Peirce was mainly interested in these analytic parts, but I am not going to examine these results of the EG. In order to get to our definition of "recognizing" we have to examine more closely the synthetic "doing" of the EG, whose first character is that they give us "evidence."

Clearly diagrams cannot do it alone. In the same text, "Prolegomena for an Apology to Pragmatism" (ibid., 313–30), Peirce explains that diagrammatic icons could not give evidence if they did not involve a symbol of which they are the interpretants. Peirce explains the way in which we pass from a diagram (transformand diagram) to another (transformate diagram) according to a scheme (the Kantian word is used to signify the combination of diagrammatic icon and initial symbolic interpretant) through his analytic semiotic theory. Thanks to this theory, we understand that the second diagram is somehow involved in the first (ibid., 318–19). But, setting aside the analytic semiotic explanation, what we observe in diagrams is a generality. As we have seen, universals live in singulars.

Besides evidence, here we have a second important character, which belongs to any mathematical analysis: mathematics has an enormous power of generalization (Peirce 1997, 131). If we analyze this property, we will find that it is due to what Peirce calls an "hypostatic abstraction," the logical tool through which we pass "from 'good' to 'goodness' and the like" (*EP2*, 270n), and we consider this abstraction as an object.[20] So the abstraction that results from the diagrams, both in mathematics and in EG, provides this power of generalization. But how does it become real? Generalization happens in "doing" or "scribing" those diagrams. If the generalization is the analytic result of the diagrams, diagrams are the synthetic happening of generals. "Recognizing" is part of this synthetic "happening" and should have the same characters: evidence and generalization.

## *3.1 Recognizing an Identity: The Multidimensional Continuum and the Line of Identity*

Recognizing always implies an object: recognizing something. The easiest way to view this recognition is through identity (this could and should get more complicated afterwards). "Recognizing something" means to acknowledge an identity as far as semiotics and critical logic are concerned. We have to remember that the identity we are looking for is not a plain correspondence A=A, which according to Peirce is only a degenerate form of the real identity A=B (*NEM4*, 328). Identities are always passing through changes. A=A is the static correspondence drawn from the set-theoretical definition of multitudes and it is a simplification of a "more primitive" form of relation A=B (ibid., 325). The moving picture of our reasoning has to reach for the "real" case of identity.

Given our diagrams with their power of evidence and generalization, how can they help us understand our "recognizing an identity"? In EG we find exactly the same problem well stated in the beta part, corresponding to first order logic. If we want to build a predicate logic we have to state some identity that in symbolic logic we express by quantifiers. The line of identity is the tool crafted to represent the existential quantifier. But, as we already know, the identity we are looking for is part of a continuum of reality, and reality is not only a fixed reality, but also a changing one. That is why the line of identity should also change in the gamma graphs that try to draw a modal logic – namely, the logical representation of a changing reality.

Therefore, in order to make clear how EG can represent our "recognizing an identity through change," let us begin with the representation of continuity in EG. Then we will move forward to gamma graphs according to the semiotic aspect of EG, which is the most useful aspect for this book. The first kind of continuity, the continuity of reality, is represented by the sheet of assertion; it is easily stated in the alpha part, namely in the logic of propositions. The sheet represents the universe of discourse. "It is agreed that a certain sheet, or blackboard, shall, under the name of The Sheet of

Assertion, be considered as representing the universe of discourse, and as asserting whatever is taken for granted between the graphist and the interpreter to be true of that universe" (*CP* 4.396). But the process gets more complicated when in the gamma graphs we want to represent our everyday reasoning as composed of changes and possibilities. This is why Peirce looks for a different kind of continuum – not a sheet of assertion anymore, but a plastic multi-dimensional continuum.

> You may regard the ordinary blank sheet of assertion as a film upon which there is, as it were, an undeveloped photograph of the facts in the universe ... But I ask you to imagine all the true propositions to have been formulated; and since facts blend into one another, it can only be in a continuum that we can conceive this to be done. This continuum must clearly have more dimensions than a surface or even than a solid. (*CP* 4.512)

The multidimensional continuum is more "original," and the sheet of assertion of alpha and beta parts is only a picture of this original continuum (*CP* 4.512). In this continuum we are really scribing not the propositions as they actually are, but as they might be. That is why we could think of them as marks or qualities, which cannot be numerable anymore – insofar as they are possible, they refer to the continuity that surpasses the grasping power of the sets – and will exceed any multitude (ibid. 4.514), according to our definition of "perfect continuity." On a multidimensional continuum – greater than a solid – we are not writing "assertions" anymore. This multidimensional continuum is able to represent time or "Becoming" (*NEM4*, 330).

Now that we have the tool for representing the continuum of time, namely of change, we have to look for identity. In the beta graphs, the graphical tool for identity is the line of identity that can solve the problem of quantifiers. Peirce defines the line of identity as follows: "A heavily marked line without any sort of interruption (though its extremity may coincide with a point otherwise marked) shall, under the name of a line of identity, be a graph, subject to all the conventions relating to graphs, and asserting precisely the identity of the individuals denoted by its extremities" (*CP* 4.406). The line represents the existential quantifier when it is evenly enclosed and the universal quantifier when it is oddly enclosed (Roberts 1973, 51).

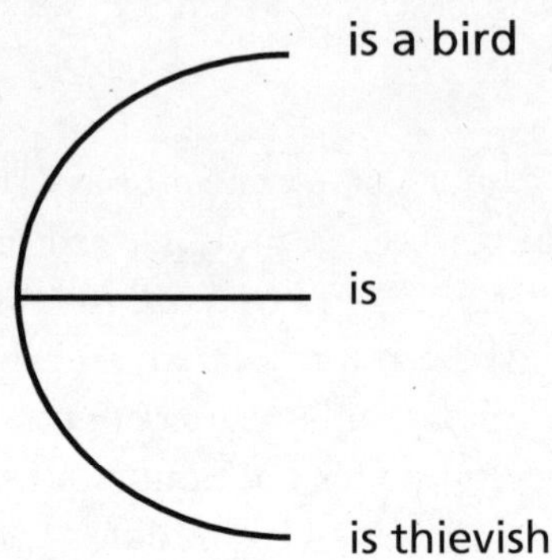


Fig 3.1: Line of identity abutting upon the same area. "Some black bird is thievish," and, of course, this can be stated in a variety of different ways: "Some thievish bird is black," "or some bird is both black and thievish" (CP 4.445, Fig. 79).

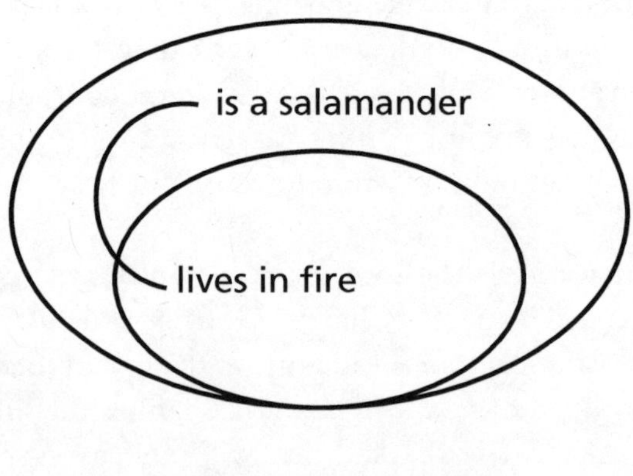


Fig 3.2: Line of identity abutting upon two different areas. "There is something which, if it be a salamander, lives in fire" (CP 4.449, Fig. 83).

But once again the definition becomes more complex when we do not have to deal with the two-dimensional sheet of assertion, but with the multidimensional plastic continuum. When we draw a line of identity on the multidimensional plastic continuum, we are representing the identity into the continuum of possibilities. Identity continues to assert the identity of the individuals denoted by its extremities, but of course the kind of identity we are drawing becomes very different.

> To say that who commanded the French in the battle of Leipzig commanded them in the final battle of Waterloo, is not merely a statement of identity: it is a statement of *Becoming*. There is an existential continuity in time between the two events. But so understood the statement asserts no Significative Identity, inasmuch as the intervening continuum is a continuum of Assertoric Truths. Now, upon a continuous line there are no points (where the line is continuous). There is only room for points – possibilities of points. Yet it is through that continuum, that line of generalization of possibilities, that the actual point at one extremity necessarily leads to the actual point at the other extremity. (*NEM4*, 330)

Identity here means the continuity of possibilities of an individual considered to be a changing object in its becoming. We will see later that this "becoming" can be seen from different aspects. Here is the general character of change that we have to make firm. This switch from using a line of identity on a sheet of assertion to instead using it on a multidimensional continuum invests the passage from an assertoric view of truth with a broader conception of truth and identity based on possibility. Identity is no longer A=A, but a non-purely-symbolizable iconic identity passing from A to B.

This switch also implies that the line of identity, when it is scribed upon a multidimensional continuum, must become *a line of teridentity*, namely a line that represents two relations of co-identity (*MS* 300, 48). One of the extremities is a loose end, an extremity of a line of identity not abutting upon another such line in another area.

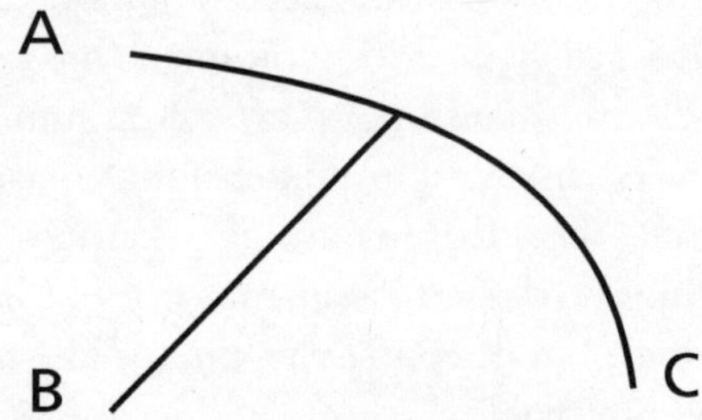


Fig 3.3: Line of teridentity (CP 4.561, Fig. 198).

Teridentity means that there are two different relations of identity that have one end and part of the line in common. As Peirce puts it, "it is identity and identity, but this 'and' is a distinct concept, and it is precisely that of teridentity" (*CP* 4.561). We need a loose end in order to guarantee the realization of a different possibility. Napoleon who lost at Leipzig is the same man who lost at Waterloo, but he might have been also the man who won at Waterloo, if the mud had not prevented his military maneuver. In this case, the loose end differs slightly from the actual end, but the line would depart earlier if the man who lost at Leipzig had decided not to invade Russia. In the gamma graphs "the line of identity must be totally abolished or rather must be understood quite differently. We must hereafter understand it to be potentially the graph of teridentity by which means there always will virtually be at least one loose end in every graph" (ibid. 4.583).[21]

Identity on a potential continuum has to present itself as the character of potentiality otherwise it would lose the capacity of representing different possible ends. A loose end means that we know identity as a continuity, but we do not know at which point it would stop, and whether it might have been different from the one we have. We have to allow for the possibility that brute existence will be different, since we are not representing actuality but potentiality.[22] Finally, the line of identity has a direction or an aim, because we draw it starting from one point and ceasing at another.[23] But this teleological characteristic will show its pertinence when we apply our logical pattern to personal identity.

### 3.2 *Mathematical and Semiotic Characteristics*

This is the tool Peirce crafted to define analytically the kind of identity we are dealing with in our different types of reasoning. But in order to grasp the synthetic view of identity, it is not EG's logical analytic use that is needed. The interesting features of the line of identity and teridentity come from Peirce's sporadic comments on its nature and meaning.

The first comment is that the line of identity, and a fortiori the line of teridentity, is another "perfect continuum" along with the multidimensional continuum of assertion. But what does it mean? "Identity means continuity, not necessarily in Place, nor in Date, but in what I may call aspect, i.e. a variety of presentation and representation" (*MS* 300, 46–7).

The line of identity is the continuity of any presentation and representation of an aspect of an individual.[24] Time and space are just two of the possibilities of these representations, even though probably the most important ones. If identity is a continuum, how can it respect the characters of reflexivity, generality, modality, and transitivity?

Before focusing on a definite answer, examining the elements that compose this line of identity will help us trace the physiognomy of the continuity of the line of identity. What is the line of identity from a semiotic point of view? According to Peirce, the line is a "perfect sign," meaning it equally blends almost all the signs. It is a general (a law) but it identifies individuals (index) in an iconic way (icon) (*CP* 4.448). Every aspect of it is important: the symbolic level allows any replica of the line to be a general interpretation grasping individuals; the indexical level marks it starting from one finite point and ending up at another one; while the iconic level – the more important one from the standpoint of this discussion – makes the line appear as "nothing but a continuum of dots, and the fact of the identity of a thing, seen under two aspects, consists merely in the continuity of being in passing from one apparition to another" (ibid.).

Why is the iconic level the most important one? Because, according to Peirce, it shows "the Forms of the synthesis of the elements of thought" (ibid. 4.544). Signs always represent an object by selecting a certain aspect in its abstract, vague form.[25] Icons, working by similarity, represent this form in a mental or physical diagram. It follows, then, that icons bring the first form and the first feeling that an object "emanates" (*MS* 637, 30). In icons we can see the form of the relations that an object might have, if it were realized according to certain conditions. That is why to those forms we owe mathematics' synthetic capacity, with its huge power of evidence and generalization: they manifest the possibility of any relation that the (dynamic) object may have and would have, if realized. "Icons can represent nothing but Forms and Feelings. That is why Diagrams are indispensable in all Mathematics from Vulgar Arithmetic up, and in Logic are almost so" (*CP* 4.544). Icons exist only as an image in the mind (ibid. 4.447). They "merely suggest the possibility of that which they represent, being percepts minus the percussivity of percepts" (*NEM4*, 317–18). Icons have the nature of "an appearance, and as such, strictly speaking, exist only in consciousness" (*CP* 4.447), regardless of actual existence. So the icons that furnish form and feeling to the line of identity, ontologically speaking, are possibilities. Peirce sums up the complex iconic nature of the line of identity, also hinting at a comparison between the logical tool and what it means in our reasoning (almost from a psychological point of view).

> Now, for the continuity of the line of identity. This being one-dimensional, or dyadic (i.e. running two ways only) should represent an internal or mental continuity; and being definitely marked should iconize a continuity of attention! But the heavy line is generated by the continuity of the different places of a heavy dot, which is the appropriate icon of an individual object in a Universe of continuous co-being; and therefore the continuity of the line is, best, the Icon of the continuity in attentive observation of an individual object. (*MS* 300, 42)

We are now ready to verify our four characteristics of continuity. The line of identity is made of interpreted icons and as such is made of possibilities whose realizations are connected by a general rule. It is exactly like the "perfect" or "real" continuum described above, according to the properties of modality and generality. The loose end guarantees that this possibility would be open – even if the two brutally cut ends seem to impose a certain kind of actuality. And it also guarantees the fullness of reflexivity: all parts of the line, including the ends, are possibilities that might be realized according to a general law. The "perfect" continuum of the line of (ter) identity is written upon the "perfect" multidimensional continuum, and every part of the two of them shares the same nature.

What about transitivity? Every single dot actualized on the multidimensional continuum realizes a possibility according to the general law, and might have a different branch – the loose end – as a different actualization of the same possibility. So there is a passage from possibility to necessity through actuality, and even a passage from necessity to actuality. Possibility as such cannot be denied, since in the realm of possibilities the principle of contradiction does not hold. The translation of modalities in terms of vagueness, determination, and generalization is easy to see: identity is a progressive determination tending toward a generalization (tending to identify forever the loser of Leipzig and the loser of Waterloo).

## *3.3 Unifying "Identity" and "Recognizing an Identity"*

Those technical passages help us to understand how Peirce thought that EG could express both identity and recognition of identity. Identity is neither a dialectic nor a permanence of characters. Identity is a possible continuity of possible qualities ("aspects" in Peirce's previous definition) that become more and more determinate during the development (the "becoming") expressed by the continuum within which they are inscribed. In other words, identity is a revisable development of the (dynamic) object through changes of time and space, or whatever aspect of the continuum we could imagine, or a kind of reality indeterminate but determinable in different singularities that would become necessary in the long run.

Peirce was proud of having found a way to represent all of that in his iconic logic ("my chef d'oeuvre"), and in so doing, of putting to work the common sense idea of identity into the modal logic of the gamma graphs. But how can this representation of identity also be the representation of "recognizing an identity"? The most intriguing part of Peirce's theory is that it allows for the unification of "identity" and "recognizing an identity." It does this by virtue of the practical "scribing" on the sheet of assertion, viz., on the multidimensional continuum. "Recognizing an identity" in EG means to draw a line of identity between two points, knowing that there is always a different, loose possibility. It is a "re-cognition" because our drawing of the line is not only a cognition of a single point, but also an acceptance of the original identity of the two points: they are distant but the same. And the drawing itself is our recognizing; in EG there is no recognition without the actual drawing of the line, exactly as there is no triangle without its image. It can be a mental or a virtual act, but it has to be a kind of diagram within a general interpretation.[26] It is what we call a mathematical gesture. In other words: identity coincides with the operation of recognizing an identity, thus respecting the deepest insight of pragmatism that considers objects and thoughts as parts of the same "experience." If the problem of identity were disconnected from the "recognizing," the two alternative ways of understanding identity as permanence of characters (or substance) or dialectic of characters would be unavoidable. In both cases identity becomes a supreme concept: either we understand it statically (the Porphirius tree is possibly the most complete representation of the consequences of this kind of comprehension)[27] or dynamically (Hegel). Sure enough, there is also a permanence of something in this pragmatist proposal: a part of experience lingers while its representation evolves. As in the case of persons, any part of experience can change and remain recognizable at the same time. In chapter 6 I will better illustrate this example.

On the other hand, the model of recognizing certainly implies a sort of dialectic. There is a dialectic in transforming some aspect of a vague experience that we want to represent into an actual line, and then a dialectic to conceive this actuality as an element of a general form of representation of which it constitutes an embodiment. Here we have a phenomenological dialectic, as in Hegel.

However, this dialectic is easier: it comprehends the passage among the different phenomenological, semiotic, and logical stages of vague ideas, concrete existential actions, and habits of thought and action. I will explore these items fully in the next chapter.

Here I want us to note that this sort of determination is not a "denial" or an "opposition" of the initial experience. In its turn, the generalization is not a superior moment that includes the two previous moments. The determination that happens in mathematical gestures is an evolution more than a dialectic – and it belongs to the same mathematical gesture, which has to be conceived as a unity. The similarity between these two phenomenologies in their tripartition and in the function that the three parts have is striking. But the difference reflects a crucial divergence: while Hegel aims for the entirety of the concept, my pragmatist proposal aims for the unity of experience – of which concept is one aspect – and to the verification of the experience itself. In other words, while the German thinker's dialectic stems from concepts and aims to knowledge or science, a pragmatist view of synthesis like the one I am proposing stems from experience and aims to another more general and embodied experience. Hegelian dialectic is a process of fulfillment of concepts, while this dialectic is a development of experience.[28]

The unity of both identity and recognizing an identity in EG was enough for Peirce because his project was about representing analytically our synthetic reasoning, including the reasoning we usually perform when we recognize objects that change all the time. Since my project differs from his, insofar as I want to synthetically understand our synthetic reasoning as "recognizing identity through changes," I have to find what shares the very characteristics of the line of teridentity in our everyday reasoning. We learned from EG the properties we are looking for: evidence, generalization, perfect continuity (reflexive, transitive, possible, and general), equal blending of icons, indices, and symbols – a phenomenological structure of determination and generalization.

# 4

# A New Tool: Complete Gesture

The previous chapter presented a new pattern for synthetic reasoning, one based on recognition of identity through changes. This pattern looks at any synthetic reasoning as an accomplished action. The accomplished action is one in which we establish the identity of two objects – or rather, the identity of aspects of objects at two different points within the continuity of change. Synthesis, therefore, ought to be understood as a kind of comparison in changes. Such a comparison is expressed as the determination of experience from a vague state to a general one through a singular act. We said that this pattern shows a development within a unitary action and not a dialectic.

I showed that Peirce himself hinted toward this kind of reasoning while he was building the system of EG. The graphs correspond to this new view of synthesis more in the semiotic and philosophical considerations they afford than in the development of logical formulas. We have seen that – almost unknowingly – Peirce represented his analytic of reasoning synthetically. He used mathematical gestures and graphs, and he gave them enormous explicative power. Their rationale is to bring universals into singulars, and we have seen what it means as far as logical identity is concerned: to recognize an identity means to draw a continuous line that is a "perfect continuum" in a multidimensional plastic continuum. Moreover, we have seen that the study of EG singled out four characteristics that any logical/epistemic tool must have in order to accomplish the same synthetic function: evidence, generalization, perfect continuity, and an equal blending of icons, indices, and symbols.

What does the line of identity mean in everyday life and reasoning? What does it refer to in our common-sense synthetic logic? As said previously, there are several passages in which Peirce compares the line of identity and the continuum to different psychological tools (feelings, volition, and cognition), but we are not concerned with this sort of metaphorical comparison here (*MS* 300, 42). Now, we have to single out an epistemic tool for our everyday reasoning, one that allows us to study the defined synthetic reasoning in its synthetic performance. We are not looking for a mere comparison or metaphor, but for the actual realization of that synthetic reasoning in our everyday experience. This kind of reasoning should show the flesh and bones of our synthetic paths, as the pragmatic maxim and the hypothetical detour do (to mention just two important tools that Peirce discovered but did not express in a synthetic pattern). According to our paradigm, synthetic reasoning is a reasoning that recognizes identity within a change. So the question is this: how do we reason synthetically in our everyday reasoning? Or, in other words, how do we recognize identities of the type A=B? More existentially, how do we perform the development of experience from a vague state to a general state – our way to synthetize aspects of experience?

## 1. GESTURES AND COMPLETE GESTURES

What are the synthetic ways of reasoning in which we usually use universals in singulars? What are the ways of recognizing identities that display the characters of a "perfect sign" and "perfect continuity"? The answer has to do with the synthetic tools Peirce himself used. Exactly like mathematical gestures and graphs, our synthetic reasoning is a "gesture." Mathematical gestures and graphs are parts of a broader synthetic tool, which is gesture in general. Using this term, my theory will confirm an important idea from the twentieth-century French philosophy of mathematics. In particular Cavaillès, Desanti, Châtelet, Longo, and Alunni referred to gesture as the tool for a non-analytic reasoning.[1]

What is a gesture in general? Gesture is any performed act with a beginning and an end that carries a meaning (from *gero* = I bear, I carry on).[2] Meaning will be pragmatically understood as the cluster of conceivable effects of an experience. Generally speaking, we can say we clarify something when we transform our vague, familiar comprehension into a habit of action, not when we have a good definition. Peirce made this clear with his three degrees of clarity of an idea (familiarity, definition, habit of action) (*EP1*, 124–32). And, even more generally, when we say that a person's understanding of something needs to be tested, we mean that the effectiveness of reasoning will be shown only in its synthetic features. Namely, only when a person can show that they can recognize the identity of two representations or that they can perform the operation that illustrates that identity do we find reasoning "effective."

But we are not seeking just any gesture. Some gestures are only reactions. All gestures carry meaning, but they do not necessarily serve to recognize an identity fully. So, while any gesture is meaningful, not every gesture shows a synthetic reasoning; or rather, they all show synthetic reasoning at different levels. Only a certain kind of gesture shows the structure of synthetic reasoning at a level that can be noticed. There are some gestures, therefore, that are so little synthetic that one usually says there is no syntheticity in them. During this chapter, the study of more exemplary gestures will lead us to understand the structure of all gestures, grasping the feeble syntheticity that they carry out.

In order to understand syntheticity we have to look for a "perfect" or a "complete" gesture, a gesture that respects all the characters we found following EG: evidence, generalization, continuity in a Peircean sense, and an equal blending of kinds of signs. I will mainly illustrate the last two items because they are the structural characteristics that would also lead to the first ones. To these characteristics I will add an equal blending of kinds of phenomena. I will use the naming "complete" in order to avoid any moralist accent of the word "perfect"; however, here "perfect" and "complete" are actually synonymous. Confirming the anti-dichotomic attitude of the entire pragmatist movement, the description of complete gestures will overtake the dichotomic separation between comprehension and communication of meaning, also showing in this unity one of the important changes of conception that the era of new information and communication technologies is manifesting.[3]

The definition of a complete gesture is phenomenological and semiotic. Let us start with semiotics. We should call a complete gesture one that has all the semiotic elements almost equally (or "densely," as I will explain later on) blended together. For a gesture to be complete it has to be a *general* law (one with a general meaning) that generates replicas (symbol); it is *actual* when it indicates its singular object (index); and it expresses different *possibilities* of forms and feelings (icon).[4] The three semiotic characteristics describe what a complete gesture is and should be: creative because of possible forms and feelings, singular and unrepeatable in its individuality, and recognizable for its unity and conformity to an established pattern that the gesture itself tends to realize. This tendency to be determined is a teleological orientation that will be important in our following study on this rational tool.

We should complete this semiotic level with a tripartition from the point of view of the "doctrine of elements" (*EP2*, 350). According to what has been said in the previous chapter, this level is based on the division among vagueness (indetermination by the utterer), determination, as well as generality (indetermination by the interpreter). A complete gesture, like the line of identity, has to display a path that progressively determines meaning going from vagueness to generality.

In turn, this classification also reflects those phenomenological relations that Peirce called firstness, secondness, and thirdness in order to express the fundamental relation of a phenomenon of experience with itself, with another phenomenon, and with a relationship that presides over any kind of generality. Complete gestures must also be complete on the phenomenological ground: the equal (or dense) blending of semiotics means also equal (or dense) blending of phenomenological aspects. If translated into a gesture, those phenomenological aspects imply a pure idea or a pure feeling (firstness), a physical act that will involve a reaction, that is, at least two objects – or subjects, as we know there is no difference in a pragmatist account of experience – (secondness), and a generality (thirdness).

Clear examples of complete gestures are liturgies in every religion, public and private rites (every social gathering has its own rites), public and private actions that establish an identity, and of course artistic performances and hypothesizing experiments. In these types of complete gestures we observe the general structure of complete gestures themselves and the pattern of syntheticity as we described it. If you think of forms of baptism in any religion or ceremonies such as coronations, oaths, or funeral services, then you get a good image of what a complete gesture is in religion and public rites. As anthropology explains, ritual gestures fill up everyday life in education, love, and death. A gesture is not just one action among many others. It is the expression of meaning embodied in one person at a singular moment, and it tends to become a habit for the person and eventually for the generalized person, the people, or the tradition.[5]

A good example for private complete gestures is more difficult to establish because the privacy prevents sharing them. However, I will explain one public-private complete gesture that is to be understood in an educational way. Some Italian mountaineers keep this old habit: if a young person makes a stone roll during a hike due to inattention, he/she has to carry the stone for some meters in order to remember how dangerous his/her inattention could have been and could be to other people. It is a private-public complete gesture created to link the person, the stone, and the educational purpose in an original way – namely, in an individual action (in *an* experience, Dewey used to say)[6] that has to be evident and generalizable.

At the scientific level, the first time an experiment is finished it is clearly a complete gesture. Rutherford's landmark gold foil experiment linked physical atoms and the golden device, in an original way and at a determinate moment, in order to discover the structure of atoms. Writing Hamlet (or any other creative moment in any sort of art) is a complete gesture that links imagination to some specific forms of experience, to the actual mechanism of the plot, and to the end or the general purpose of the story (even no purposefulness is a purpose).

In all of the examples I have considered, there is a phenomenological path that establishes a threefold relationship in which two objects are related according to a general law (to which they tend in a teleological way) in order to embody in a determinate way some possible ideas. In turn, the embodiment enhances the general law itself and the path of determination that proposes, fosters, or strengthens a habit of action. Besides, this relationship singles out the objects (by indices) according to an interpretative path (symbols) that helps in determining and in transforming some "form" connected to the two objects (icon). The determination reinforces or proposes the interpretation or meaning.

While more examples could be provided and the following chapters will point to some further examples, my goal in this chapter is to more fully articulate the phenomenological and semiotic structure of complete gesture. In order to do this, it is necessary to point out that the phenomenological and semiotic paths reveal an internal tendency to a goal, a *telos*. The telos is the embodied meaning itself. In fact, this complex structure is teleologically oriented from initial vagueness to meaningful generality through a singular event. The telos means neither pre-determination nor obligation: the telos is the tendency to generalize that every gesture requires as such for the dynamic of its elements (thirdness and symbols). The idea that purpose decides meaning is at the very heart of pragmatism. The finalism of pragmatism implies a strong semiotic or logical account that precludes any arbitrariness. Why should every continuity imply teleology? Continuity evolves ontologically through the transition among modalities, but from an epistemological standpoint it develops through our semiotic and logical path. Otherwise it would be utterly incomprehensible.

Now, teleology is profoundly implied in the conception of sign. As is well known, according to Peirce the threefold structure of sign is composed by object/representamen/interpretant. On a basic level signs show a final causation through interpretants. However, a closer look reveals that they behave that way because of their symbolic level, which has a tendency to be interpreted. This symbolic tendency amounts to a final cause (Hulswit 2002, 156; Gava 2014, 112–14). So final causation or teleology is part of the "speculative grammar"[7] of our logical process. Sure enough, it is a process that has a direction (anisotropy), but this direction is intrinsic to the semiotic process, which is the driving energy of any meaningful process. It is the final idea that compels the direction of signs.[8] In EG the importance of this tendency is represented by the inward direction necessary to read graphs (endoporeutic method) and by the clockwise order to read lines of identity. Not surprisingly this is the symbolic interpretation that EG require, which differentiates them from every other logical graph (*CP* 4.420–1).

However, the same capacity of generalization implies the capacity for re-performance (which is different from repetition, as we will see later on); and a real reperformance involves a revision of all the elements of the gestures and their sequence. Completion requires this revision necessarily: we always have to revise the vague universal of experience that we want to embody by selecting a particular aspect of it. This aspect can also be slightly different from other performances of the same gesture; we can decide on a different determination of the gesture in order to change – to increase or decrease, to ameliorate or to degrade – the generality of the meaning we are embodying.

In the next chapter, personal identity will be discussed as being a result of the teleological drive of complete gestures. For now, having stated the elements of complete gestures, let us return to the "equality" that is such a decisive part of their description.

## *1.1 Incomplete and Complete Gestures*

What does equal blending mean? One possible interpretation is quantitative: in this case you have to put some percentage of each kind of sign or phenomenon. This procedure will result in a sort of mechanical structuralism, far away from Peirce's organic conception of signs. It is the sort of analysis of perfection that in the movie Dead Poets Society (1989) Professor Keating makes fun of: a calculus of meters, rhymes, figures of speech on the one side and contents on the other, that should give the "area of greatness" of the poems. Of course, this is not what we need here. It is necessary to avoid a quantitative reading of this equality. In fact, a quantitative understanding will lead to the analytic part-whole scheme that I had wanted to avoid, and that is far from pragmatists' direction of thought. Following a suggestion by Zalamea,[9] we can read equality in terms of density in order to escape a metric understanding of this characteristic. In this way reality appears as a web of relationships. Complete gestures are points in which this web is particularly dense as far as semiotic characters are concerned.[10] We can use "dense" for "equal" and "loose" for "unequal."

So far, I can reach a negative description of it. We can say what the unequal or loose blending means from a phenomenological and a semiotic point of view. The list of inequalities or loose presences coincides with the list of incomplete gestures, actions that carry a meaning, and somehow still synthetize, but do not reach the full syntheticity of the identity A=B, namely the full expression of a universal in a singular action. The lists will exemplify what I mean. However, they are not exhaustive. Further studies can emend or clarify them. My point is to make clear that the completion of gesture is the original form of comprehension/communication and any other form can be derived from it. This primacy is due to the primacy of syntheticity over analyticity.[11]

Starting from phenomenology, we can say that when secondness and thirdness are weak (it is impossible that they are missing completely, otherwise we would no longer be talking about gestures), gesture remains a "pure idea" or a "pure feeling." It is an *ideation*. When only thirdness is weak, gesture is an *exhibition*. The object of experience is shown in a singular point but there is no further habit of action that develops from it. When secondness is weak a gesture becomes a *projection*. When firstness and thirdness are weak a gesture becomes a clash or a *reaction*, a single response without new ideas or feelings and with no possibility for further realization. When firstness is weak, a gesture based on secondness and thirdness becomes a habit without novelty, a habit in Wittgenstein's sense of the word (like driving a car when one has long ago learned how). I will use the Kantian word of *schematization* to describe this type of gesture. When both firstness and secondness are weak, a gesture becomes an *abstraction*.

As for the semiotic mixture of elements, when indices and symbols are weak in a gesture, this latter becomes a stream of images (*imagination*). When symbols are weak, gestures are *information*; they work like living captions. When indices are weak, we have formal models (*modeling*). When icons and symbols are weak, gestures are only *indications*, communication of reference.

When icons are weak we have plain *repetition*. When both icons and indices are weak we have a *conceptualization*.

We can tell from the following figures that none of these incomplete gestures has a negative role. They are still meaningful actions with a beginning and an end, and they bear a meaning. In-completion means only that the way in which they are gestures does not reach full, dense synthetization, or embodiment of universals, or recognition of identity through change. They hint at this recognition and sometimes direct toward it, without reaching a full meaningfulness. Here full means evident and completely generalizable, with the four characteristics of generality, modality, transitivity, and reflexivity that the study of continuity brought into the open. In particular, phenomenology of complete and incomplete gestures accounts for events that display a particular form.

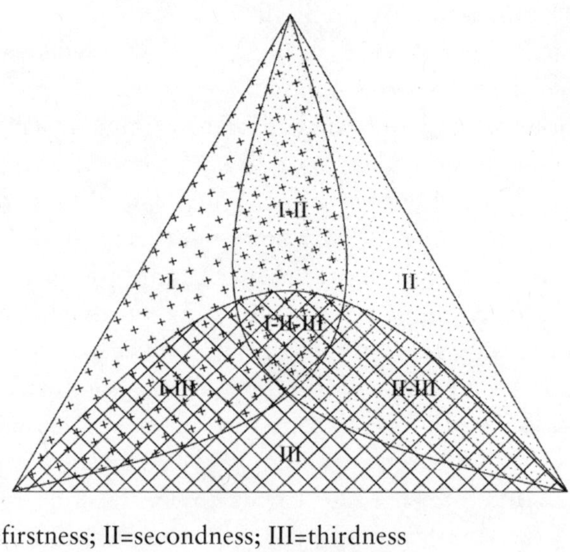


Fig 4.1: I=firstness; II=secondness; III=thirdness

*Ideation* (I) is an action that lives for its own sake in the realm of possibilities, without material clashes with other realities or patterns of generalization. Dreams and daydreaming fall within this category. *Reaction* (II) is an action that responds to another one *almost* mechanically ("almost" because we are always talking actions that bear a meaning, and so doing, they cannot be totally mechanic).

*Abstraction* (III) is an action that has an overwhelming prevalence of thirdness. Establishing a law is this sort of operation.
*Exhibition* (I–II) is an action that presents some aspect of its object, without claiming any further pattern of realization than the actual manifestation: a painting with a label under it or a merely formal indication or introduction.
*Projection* (I–III) is an action that plans or models or fosters further relationships without the actual happening of their occurrence. Thinking on a project, pondering, and contemplating fall under this heading.
*Schematization* (II–III) is an action that puts singular actual objects within a scheme without inquiring about their nature and aspects (forms) furthermore. Familiar habits in the usual sense of the word – like driving a car when one is used to it – fall within this category.
*Complete gesture* (I–II–II), according to the definition given in section 1.

Semiotic categories correspond to phenomenological ones as far as the communication of meaning is concerned. Notwithstanding this correspondence, they cannot be considered a subset of the previous categories because of the different nature of their subject matter.

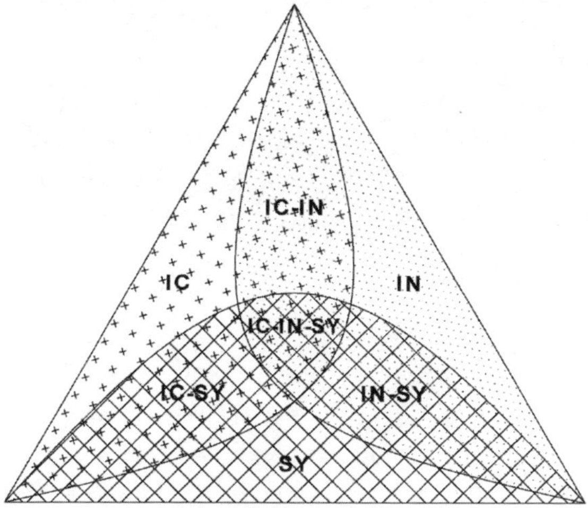


Fig 4.2: IC = icon; IN = index; SY = symbol

*Imagination* (IC) is an action in which icons display the form of the object without looking for interpretation or for the actual occurrence in which the embodiment of the image will take place.
*Indication* (IN) is an action that transmits meaning as a reference. When we refer to a person who is neither present nor known to the people we are talking to, we are indicating him/her.
*Conceptualization* (SY) is an action through which we transform thinking into concepts.
*Information* (IC–IN) is an action that fixes the reference between the form of the object and the situation. "Gesturing" in the more ordinary sense of the word is part of this category as is, for example, the news on mass media.[12]
*Modeling* (IC–SY) is an action that transmits meaning by deepening the form of experience from which it stems and its interpretative pattern without caring for its actual singular realization. A project in the usual sense of the word is a good example.
*Repetition* (IN–SY) is an action that conveys fixed meaning without inquiring the form of the object anymore. Stereotypes and orders belong to this category as well as repetition (by heart) of something. Repetition is still useful to synthetize meaning because it is still a (incomplete) gesture. However, copying is not a gesture anymore.
*Complete gesture* (IC–IN–SY), according to the definition given in section 1.

The list does not exhaust – nor is it my aim to exhaust – the many kinds of gestures, which will have to be sorted out and studied by those who will adopt the philosophy of gesture as their leading guide. For example, using Peirce's kinds of signs (59.046) we should have a much more numerous list of gestures. Besides, other classifications of signs can be used if the iconic/indexical/symbolic pattern is respected.

All properties form a "complete" unity because if any part is weak, gestures miss some important part of comprehension/communication. In a way, they always become formal. "Formality" does not imply a lack of utility or a moral negative judgment. It only means that complete gestures are composed of possible meanings and possible realizations through a specific form that requires a singular individual. Every pure possibility becomes more and more determinate as the gesture is more complete. When any part of a gesture is not fully realized, its meaning can regress to bare possibility, or lose its specificity or novelty. The gesture itself remains incomplete. It is what we call a formal gesture, and formal gestures can be mental gestures like reasoning, creative gestures like literary works, or artistic gestures like painting, sculpture, or musical creation. There are also formal gestures in religion, in love, and in death.

In our study of complete gestures, we find that perfect continuity involving both generalities and singularities that Peirce was unsuccessfully striving for on analytic grounds. Does the gesture respect the criterion of perfect continuity, namely generality, modality (plasticity), transitivity, and reflexivity? We have already seen that gestures carry a possible and vague meaning that progressively gets determinate until a habit (in Peirce's sense of the word) is established. So we can easily find in this movement generality, modality, and transitivity. Moreover, the possibility of learning a new gesture – like a new language (which is the performance of a gesture as anybody verifies when learning a foreign language) – or a gesture replacing the one we habitually perform corresponds to the open possibilities of the loose end in EG. Completion also implies a constant deepening of possibilities. This is why repetition is not a complete gesture: repetition is a performance that does not deepen the novelty of iconic forms anymore. Therefore, if the tendency of a gesture goes from vagueness to generality, it is also true that the structure of gesture comprehends a continuous swinging back to vagueness in order to iconically represent the vague universals we want to embody (i.e. we can perform the same purification bath in many ways, modeling slightly different versions of the same meaning).

As we have seen, this account does not mean that incomplete gestures are useless. Many of them carry important meaning in their own way. According to the definition of synthesis that I gave, in which synthesis means to acquire something new and non-conceptual that increases intension, these incomplete gestures synthetize to a very weak degree; they can fashion or recognize identity through changes, but only in a very weak way. In other words, incomplete gestures cannot fully embody universals into singulars that propose or enhance generals. The effect is that their comprehending/communicating power is limited but not in vain.

In technical terms we can say that they lose some of the required characteristics for completion. Sometimes they stop being evident or generalizable, or they lack some of the fundamental properties of continua. One of them is *generality* itself: if a gesture misses generality, it cannot be performed by many. *Modality* implies an action that is not tied only to actuality: to the degree that a gesture is not complete, this effort to adhere to actuality increases. In the case of information for example, it only transmits meaning as a reference. *Transitivity* indicates the transition among modalities. When a gesture is incomplete, internal transition is not fluid. Examples of this include gestures that remain images, gestures that cannot return to possibility for a new embodiment (schematization or repetition), and gestures that remain pure information. If a gesture does not hold *reflexivity*, it is incomplete insofar as its parts do not convey the same meaning of the whole to which they belong, and they do not require the other elements necessarily. Examples of this lack of reflexivity are ordinary actions in which meaning is disconnected from actual doing. If I walk while I talk on the phone, the two phenomenological elements (1) the actual walking and (2) the general meaning I am conveying through words are separate from one another. The semiotic indices of my body and my talk – and the symbolic meaning of both – are severed. Also in less incomplete gestures such as those listed above, the unreflexivity works in the same way: the weak element in any category shows how that element does not tend to generate full generality or full meaningfulness.

In positive terms, we can ask the following: what are we performing in every complete gesture? On the one hand, a singular act performed by a singular person (or persons) is embodying a general rule according to a certain interpretation. On the other hand, the person is here creating a "necessary" habit. The re-performance of the form involves a replica of the feelings, and it tends to foster a habit of action. Possibilities become acts and acts want to become habits or necessities. As a matter of fact the same gesture can be made by many different people, but it becomes actual only when a singular person is actualizing it – and only for that person does it tend to become a general habit. In its turn, generality itself is modified by that singular action that can propose, increase, or foster new ways of old habits or new habits, as far as we can call something "new" (absolute novelty is impossible). Generalization is granted by the possibility that a complete gesture is "accomplished by many"; evidence resides in the perception of that generality of meaning within an action that transforms forms through a change.

Semiotic constitution proves reflexivity exactly as it does in the line of identity of EG. Any part (law, actual realization, aspect) has the same properties of the general continuum, affording alternative possible realizations and applications of the same gesture. But any part also has to convey the pattern of relationships and meaning of the entire gesture. The complete gesture realizes the meaning, and there is no possibility of full expression of that meaning without gesture. In turn, meaning is in any part of the gesture, and it is the telos of any part as well as of the entire gesture.

### 1.2 *Complete Gesture and Different Kinds of Reasoning*

The argument we have provided follows Peirce's insight about the uncountable nature of continuity. If there is a continuity exceeding any multitude stemming from set theory, there must also be a reasoning that exceeds the analytic pattern of the set theory. Since that exceeding continuity is the original reality we refer to in our reasoning, we should find a different path of reasoning, complementary to the analytic one and in communication with it.

Our new paradigm implies that a synthetic judgment (and reasoning) is a judgment (and reasoning) that recognizes – with evidence – identity through changes. How can we perform this reasoning? We do it through complete gestures. Complete gestures – like the line of identity showed in EG – save identity through changes because of their continuous phenomenological and semiotic nature. Recalling Peirce's degrees of clarity of ideas, we could say that the degree of pragmatic maxim (meaning is the sum of all the conceivable effects of an idea) corresponds to the synthetic path. It is the embodied universal, namely the complete gesture that shows what the meaning is.

We obtain analytic and vague reasoning by differentiation. Analytic reasoning loses the identity through changes because it is concerned with breaking up the identity, as its etymology suggests (analysis from *analyo*: discomposing, breaking up). As we said, it is very useful in certain circumstances. For example, we make use of it to understand what characteristics are necessary for a complete gesture. However, analytic reasoning has another aim, one that is very profitable in many cases but perfectly useless in much of our everyday business, and sometimes also – like in the case of discoveries or assessments of meaning – in many of our scientific activities. The degree of clearness of definition corresponds to the analysis. As we know, definitions are always either too loose or too tight – namely, they lose or grasp the identity of their object. Definitions are very useful if we conceive of them as a limited way to cut and grasp experience.

A vague reasoning does not recognize an identity, but it is probably the richer state of our knowledge, the one in which our primeval beliefs and common sense originate. Of course, these beliefs are only vague, and thus are only secure within the limit of the need they point out. But sometimes, to ascertain our need is the first step toward any scientific decomposition and meaningful gesturing. I hope that further studies will find and clarify the tool which is the correspondent of complete gesture as far as a vague logic is concerned: a vague tool to understand vague reasoning (and then to analyze it). The degree of clarity of familiarity corresponds to vagueness.[13] To say we know something in a vague way does not mean to say we do not know it at all. It means that we do not know how to define it or transform its meaning into a complete gesture. However, this familiar awareness is the beginning of any definition and any gesture.

Our reasoning is thus like a swinging pendulum.[14] At one pole, there is an extreme syntheticity that is represented by complete gestures. At this pole our reasoning coincides with the performance of a complete synthetic action. On the other side of the pendulum we find the extreme analysis that is represented by formal logical analysis. Between these two poles there are intermediate levels of synthetic and analytic reasoning. As we have seen, on the synthetic side there are many degrees of incompletion of gestures in which synthesis is weaker due to the weakness of one or two of the elements of its constitution. And on the analytic side, classic logic and epistemic analysis represent weaker stages of analytic reasoning.

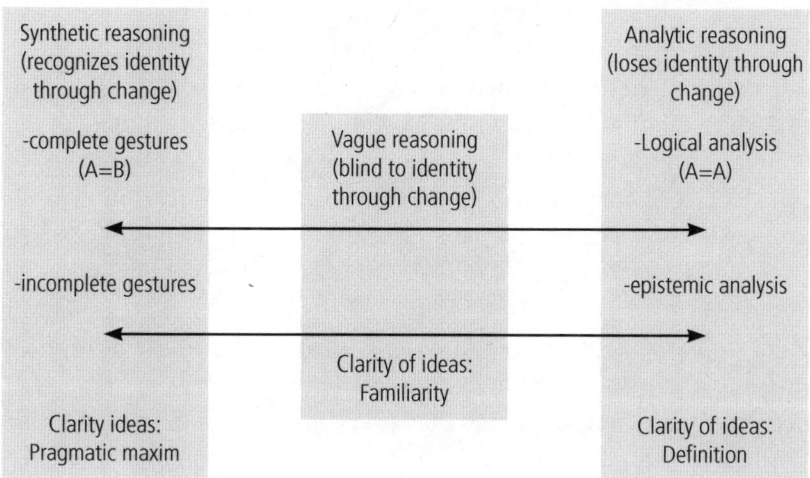


Figure 4.3: Swinging pendulum of reasoning

However, vagueness (or vague reasoning) is an intermediate kind of reasoning through which we pass from one extreme to the other. In fact, we start performing gestures by taking universals out of vagueness; when we want to translate some analytic concept into a gesture, we have to rethink its aspects, possible realizations, and laws of realization in a vague way. We do this by accepting contradictory possibilities, the plurality of realizations, and different and imprecise laws of generalization and interpretation. When we start analyzing, we have to stop and cut a concept out of our synthetic reasoning in order to isolate it and break up its identity. Stopping means to momentarily cancel the identity A=B of our synthetic reasoning in order to question it again in an analytic way. This operation passes by an erasure of the recognized identity that, for a moment, takes the meaning back to its vague state.

Is this vague state also primeval in the absolute sense of the word? Does it stem before the others? Certainly we know that synthesis precedes analysis. Breaking up concepts and experiences presupposes already synthesized concepts and experiences. However, we do not know whether this experience is received by reasoning in a synthetic or in a vague way. There are reasons for both solutions (the rationale of vague reasoning is not the topic of this book and in any case has not been studied properly). In addition, it is worth noting that what Peirce meant by vagueness is a much broader notion than what is housed under the phrase "logic of vagueness" in contemporary analytic discussion. (Even though there are connections between this pair). According to our definition from chapter 3, vagueness is a state in which identity does not matter. But just as we needed a synthetic tool in order to explore syntheticity, we need a vague tool that can be of certain help in exploring vagueness. Roberto Perry named the discipline "horotics," the logic of borders (horos), and now a tool for vagueness should also be developed in order to traverse the terrain that gives birth to both new creative syntheses and more precise analyses (Maddalena and Zalamea 2012). So far I can see that this field exists, but I cannot see a tool to inquire after it. For the time being, this book is dedicated to the complete gesture as a tool to unravel the synthetic pattern, and the next chapters are devoted to this task.

# 5

# Gestures and Creativity

In the last chapter I listed the elements that compose a complete gesture from both a phenomenological and a semiotic standpoint. In this chapter, I will specify the kind of function that complete gestures have in our knowledge. This function will offer us the opportunity to reveal some important conditions that are fundamental to the performance of a complete gesture. The specific function I am referring to can go under the heading of "creativity." Our complete gestures perform the most interesting behaviour of the human mind and, perhaps, further studies will identify them as a possible anthropological threshold or liminality. As we will see, creativity has many degrees and human beings reach the top of these degrees with complete gestures.

The topic of creativity has often been confined to aesthetics, even though the creative process is immensely important for any sort of inquiry. From a scientific perspective, explained in Peirce's account of abduction, creativity is part of the path of discovery, the point at which we formulate a new hypothesis.[1] In every sort of art, creativity covers almost the entire body of content. But as Dewey pointed out (1934) in our everyday experience, creativity is what describes our best acts in social relationships, in education, and in jobs of every kind.

Our way of looking at an occasion of synthetic reasoning based on the paradigm of complete gestures can fulfill a tendency that was present in pragmatism from the beginning. As a matter of fact, classic pragmatism was already an interesting vehicle with which to approach the topic of creativity in a way that was neither naïve nor reductive. The naïve way simply excludes creativity from the rational realm, as in Plato's *Ion* where creativity is identified with God's gift and, as such, is incomprehensible for human intellect (*Ion* 542a). The reductive conception pigeonholes creativity into the aesthetic realm where, as in the first Wittgenstein, it keeps its high normative function but – at the same time – its nonsensical status for rational processes (Wittgenstein 1984, 178–81). As we have seen, classic pragmatists had a profound understanding of the unity and the rationality of experience, so pragmatism can furnish a better explanation of what creativity is. For pragmatists, experience includes – and thus overcomes – any dichotomy: thoughts and actions, facts and values, mind and body, private and public, individual and society, physics and metaphysics. With different nuances, all classic pragmatists thought that experience contains all those items at the same time because they are part of a deeper relationship or continuity.

The new synthetic pattern and the tool of complete gesture that I introduced in the last chapters serve to supplement classic pragmatists' epistemic insights. As I said, the tool of complete gesture overcomes the distinction between comprehension and communication. From this perspective, it is worth noticing that contemporary pragmatists also show the same need, particularly when they are dealing with aesthetics.

In fact, I find the same need for a different definition and use of synthetic judgment in two of the most important pragmatist aesthetics of the last decades: Margolis' (1999) and Richard Shusterman's (1992). They both push Dewey's aesthetics toward a more synthetic pattern. Margolis' definition of artworks as "physically embodied, culturally emergent entities" and his various reflections on works of art can be extended to a more general reflection on the nature of creativity as such. He is not talking about creativity as such, but the topic is very close to it, and based on the rejection of both analytic studies (from G.E. Moore to Arthur Danto) and hermeneutics. The first one is essentialist, intuitionist, and eventually nihilist; the second one is poor, not allowing for any disciplined naturalism.

Margolis' reconstruction of aesthetics vindicates pragmatism as far as it holds a stiff historicist relativism and an altogether strong naturalism at once. Margolis accuses both old essentialist views and Danto's of not considering our perceptions and our embodied sensations as already culturally informed. In such a case, we cannot simply search for refuge in some sort of Platonism or in an analytic dissolution of our object or work of art.

The trouble with Margolis' account is that as much as this cultural embodied emergentism is proclaimed, there is no technical defense of the knowing power of perceptions – which should be the keystone of his naturalist and relativist account. It is more a manifesto than an argument. At the end we find a paradox: the works of art, like any form of knowledge, are "natural entities" of a "not-natural kind." Curiously enough Margolis' defense of cultural emergentism relies on naturalism and intentionality at the same time – but without a clear definition of the latter (that would require technique), the former becomes dubious.

Shusterman attempts to deepen Dewey's aesthetic insight, broadening Dewey's notion of experience to new fields and more democratic forms of art: everyday performances that cast a light upon our aesthetic way of living. Again, Shusterman attacks old and new forms of essentialism and elitist views of art. Contrary to Margolis, he identifies the main tool of his aesthetics in a keen use of the body.

Shusterman is right to look for a description of art that will take into account everyday aesthetic experience, and to follow and increase Dewey's attention to the corporeal dimension of our aesthetical satisfaction. Shusterman does not enter into the details of how reasoning works, and he is sometimes without awareness of the achievements that pragmatists – particularly Peirce – have made in defining interpretation/understanding/perception. Even without these pieces, Shusterman hints at a full employment of corporeal characteristics in our reasoning; but again the trouble is that he does not technically explain how our body creates knowledge.

In sum, Margolis stresses the emergency of cultural aspects in corporeal expressions and artworks, while Shusterman underlines the corporeal base of any cultural expression and artwork. To me, they both point out decisive aspects of art and of knowledge in general (and creativity in particular), and they both do not find a sufficient explanation of the way in which these aspects should be put to work. Now, we will see whether the paradigm of complete gesture that I introduced in previous chapters will support classic and contemporary pragmatists' insights about creativity and aesthetics, supplementing it with a more precise semiotic study. Moreover, the topic of creativity will allow for the background conditions of gestures to emerge.

## 1. EXPLAINING CREATIVITY THROUGH EG AND COMPLETE GESTURES

It is worth recalling that we draw our conception of complete gesture from a semiotic study of EG. EG respect all features of the mathematical continuity that is the deep root of experience as change and time. Our reasoning has to move within this changing pattern synthetizing – acquiring – new elements. This "acquisition" amounts to recognizing identity through changes, where identity has to be seen not as A=A, but as A=B, of which A=A is only a degenerate (less interesting) case (*NEM4*, 325). In other words, "acquisition" coincides with recognizing that there is a connection (the line of [ter-]identity) between two points (or objects or aspects of objects) on the same evolutionary, or changing, continuum. As we have seen, this recognition takes the phenomenological aspect of a development of experience from vagueness to generality through a singular action and the semiotic aspect of a dense blending of icons, indices, and symbols. The construction of a diagram in EG and of a complete gesture in our ordinary experience need, and coincide with, creativity. A complete gesture has to be innovative, since one has to rethink the different elements and their blending.

When we "create" something we are always performing a determinate action. In the figures of the previous chapter we have seen what an action can be when it is not determinate: ideation or projection from a phenomenological standpoint, imagination or modeling from a semiotic perspective. We refer to creation when we reach a determination through actual/existent actions. However, the action is not creative if it is not purposeful and is not a way to embody possibilities. Moreover, this embodiment of possibilities or determination of vagueness happens through dense relationships among the figuration of experience by icons, the precise referral to parts of experience by indices, and the openness to interpretation granted by symbols. In any creative action you can find these elements densely blended. This is evident for artistic creations such as paintings, music, writings, and sculptures, but it happens in the same way for scientific discoveries, and for everyday cases of creativity that can change our routine habits. This analysis of signs and phenomena is not present in Margolis' and Shusterman's accounts. In particular, the very structure of signs – representamen/object/interpretant – is at the origin of the capacity of representation to give a precise understanding of the deep intertwining of physical and cultural aspects in our (aesthetic) knowledge.

Such a semiotic definition of creativity produces an obvious question: is creativity not a perennial characteristic of every kind of sign? Sure enough, to a certain degree any semiosis is creative. On the one hand, this is clear from Peirce's "On A New List of Categories" on (*EP1*, 1–10; *W2*, 49–59): there is always a degree of interpretation in any semiotic process so that a certain original synthetic process or creativity is at work. From this perspective there is a coincidence among synthesis, semiotic process, and creativity. On the other hand, when we speak of creativity we usually think of a restricted sense of the word, namely of a special performance of this semiotic pattern. Complete gesture is this special performance that moves within a completely synthetic pattern of reasoning.

Some questions follow from this discussion. Is every complete gesture creative? Or is any creation a complete gesture? I think that the implication works in both directions. If something is a complete gesture, it will be creative, originally synthetic; if something is creative, it has to be a complete gesture, and it will have this particular dense blending of phenomenological and semiotic characteristics. There remains a difference between any degree of syntheticity (creativity broadly understood) and complete syntheticity (creativity strictly understood) just as there is a difference between any incomplete and complete gesture. This difference is due to the density of the blending of signs.

Let us sum up the different levels in which the original synthesis A=B can be understood. At the first level we are analyzing the synthetic identity A=B as Peirce was doing in the project of the gamma graphs, talking about diachronic identity (Napoleon at Leipzig and Napoleon at Waterloo). The result is the evidence and generalization with which we analytically represent the synthetic recognizing A=B.

At the second level synthetic process happens as semiosis, and its result is creativity broadly understood. Here we are recognizing an identity through change, even though this synthesis is not fully achieved. The tools of this kind of synthesis are all the incomplete gestures we listed in chapter 4. It is easy to apply that list to artworks as well. Normal semiotic syntheses such as "looking at," "listening to," and so on fall into this category. On the one hand, according to the situation, they can fall into some of the categories already listed: sometimes they underline reference so that they are indications, sometimes interpretation takes over imposing conceptualization, and so on according to all categories. On the other hand, perceptions or sensations or other semiotic acts remain partly vague. The relationship and the difference between this level of syntheticity and the pattern of vagueness or horotic reasoning should be clarified when the latter is studied adequately.

At the third level, recognition of identity through change is a complete gesture in which all the characteristics from chapter 4 belong.

| | | | | |
|---|---|---|---|---|
| Analytic pattern | Line of (ter)identity (dense blending of kinds of signs) | A=B | Specific semiosis (Existential graphs) | Evidence and generalization |
| Vague (not completely determined) synthesis | Incomplete gestures | A=B | Semiosis | Creativity broadly understood |
| Completely synthetic pattern | Complete gestures (dense blending of kinds of signs) | A=B | Specific semiosis | Creativity strictly understood |

Table 5.1: Gestures and creativity

An objection can arise at this point. As Liszka correctly observed, there is usually a distinction between discovery, invention, and artistic creativity.[2] However, if this is true in an analytic pattern, it is less true in a vague synthetic pattern, and much less in a completely synthetic pattern: synthesis precedes any analysis because it is the pattern in which experience develops. Let us remember Johannes Kepler's emblematic discovery: it is full of creative thinking made of diagrams, calculus, background aesthetical convictions, and the purpose to better understand the human and divine image of the universe (Gingerich 2011). Inventions like smartphones require a previous original synthetic thought that unites purpose of communication, electronic devices, and the idea of integrating different functions previously provided by different tools. From a synthetic perspective, inventions and discoveries do not differ from artistic creativity. The point here is to understand the inversion of the paradigm: first we reason synthetically, which despite varying levels of accomplished syntheticity is always a creative form of reasoning. Only afterward can we track distinctions in an analytic way. The distinction between discovery, invention, and artistic creativity does not describe our way of experiencing and moving through experience reasonably. It comes later as a supplement to reasoning that we have already developed.

Does the tool of complete gesture respond to the needs brought into the open by Margolis and Shusterman? I think so. The complete gesture accounts for intentionality in a pragmatistically technical way: intentionality as understood by Margolis requires psychological and ethical elements, but it is mainly an interaction among representations. Semiotics, introduced by Peirce but also emphasized by Dewey, is the technical key to understanding the reasoning happening within perceptions and sensations. Besides, as Shusterman advocated, the complete gesture involves the corporeal dimension, thanks to its secondness. Moreover, it provides a more accurate tool for evaluating works of art without surrendering to both elitism and lack of distinctions. In the same way, it weakens the difference between scientific and humanist creativity: a good scientific hypothesis and a good artistic creation can both be judged as complete gestures according to the density of their semiotic "blending."

## 2. CONDITIONS OF CREATIVITY

The creative synthetic blending of semiotic elements has some necessary conditions that I will try to spell out. I do not want to try to exhaust all such conditions here, but I will start by listing those that are surely implied in any artistic creative pattern – even though I think they apply to all kinds of complete gestures.

### 2.1 *Sub-creators*

The first condition is what, stealing the term from J.R.R. Tolkien, I will call "sub-creation" (Carpenter 1995, letter 37). Any gesture, a fortiori any complete gesture, requires an author who puts it into existence. Most thinkers during the twentieth century denied the presence of the author as such (think of new criticism, deconstructionism, Roland Barthes, Michel Foucault, the second Wittgenstein, and Rorty). On the one hand, the denial came from the dismantling proper of analytic judgment. You do not need an author if your "object" of thought is already there – "ready-made" as Dewey used to say – and you have to break it up in order to understand it better. On the other hand, hermeneutic tradition obviously overtakes this point of view, but it does not need authorship either: universal interpretation makes the distinctions of roles fade away.

Both traditions of thought underline some very important aspect of our aesthetic and creative experience. Analytic philosophy shows that there are cognitive mechanisms and patterns at work in this experience, and that these mechanisms and patterns are much richer and deeper than our intentions. Hermeneutics reveals that there is a profound co-belonging of any participant to the event of creative and aesthetic experience. Authors, texts, forms of expression, meaning, interpreter, effects of interpretation share the same common ground, which can be named as cultural tradition or, in a very special sense that Hans-Georg Gadamer pointed out, as "truth" (1960). Complete gesture is a tool that involves both insights: it furnishes a cognitive account based on phenomenology and semiotics, and explains why co-belonging is experienced.

As we have seen, the synthesis of recognizing an identity through changes requires complete gestures, and complete gestures are not simply random creatures. Whereas facts can be there by chance, complete gestures cannot be if someone does not "mean" them.[3] Complete gestures are a dense blending of signs, and blending requires an author. The author can also be the actor in some gestures, but there is no gesture without the function of the author.

What is the power of the author? He can "sub-create" the complete gesture. What is a "sub-creation"? Recalling Scotus' and Peirce's distinction between reality and existence, we can say that the author can "give reality" but not existence, or rather, not every kind of existence. We have seen that in any creative process like artistic gestures of creation, mathematical hypotheses, and scientific discoveries, the blending of signs always implies a possible idea becoming existent and even necessary. But what kind of reality do we create? Of course we are not at all speaking of creation *ex nihilo*. We reshape in a new way a long path of concepts, ideas, and materials. In a pragmatist way we could say that we reshape "experience" broadly understood. The nature and limits of this reshaping will emerge as we discuss further modalities in the way Peirce himself treated them. However, we should also not forget that there really is something new that emerges in the reshaping itself. This reshaping of experience is to be taken into account from an ontological perspective, so that there is some deep sense in which we use the expression "to give reality." I will not work out this point in this book, because it will have too many broad ontological implications that need further study. Instead I will stick to the epistemological connection that the topic of creativity raises, postponing the ontological issue for further research.

As for creativity, there is no problem either in thinking of these realities that we create as possibilities or in thinking of them as necessary habits. Recalling what I said in chapter 3, according to Peirce possibility is the realm in which the principle of contradiction does not hold; anything might work, even though there are criteria of limitation. Our creative gestures generally hold any possible and plausible blending of signs.

Necessity is the realm in which the principle of the excluded third does not hold so that something that is beyond the binary A or not-A can work. Certainly, this statement applies to *de dicto* necessities, but it means that there is some reality that goes beyond any existent thing we can affirm or deny at this moment.[4] All generals have this kind of reality. Our complete gestures share this sort of generality. An invented character of a play or of a novel, or a certain kind of drawing, or even a scientific theory becomes necessary, far away from any affirmation or negation by any person. "Real" in this case means something that does not depend on what is affirmable or deniable at this moment, neither by a person nor by a certain number or even by a majority of people. Herman Melville's Captain Ahab, Jackson Pollock's "Autumn Rhythm (Number 30)" (but also Kepler's ellipses and even numbers) are realities in this sense. We created them but they became independent of what we think of them.

Existence is a more difficult issue. Can we give existence? If the term "create" is understood as "creation of matter *ex nihilo*" we cannot. We can give a different form (and feeling) to matter, and we can choose to use existent forms and feelings in a new way. Namely, we can change the law of interpretation under which our existent material will be understood. Let us think of an everyday object displayed in a museum as a work of art: we change its interpretation by putting it in a different place, but we cannot give existence to matter of any kind.

Certainly, in a sense we can put into existence some forms and feelings – but this only means that we can arrange existent matter in a certain way. We cannot create the physical body of Captain Ahab, but we can put his form into the ink of our pen, writing him down forever. Writing is a kind of gesture that has its secondness and its indexical part in the act of putting the ink (also the virtual one) on a sheet. So the indexical part of our gesture has to deal with existence, but only in this derived form. We cannot give a corporeal existence to Captain Ahab. We can write his shape or reshape his presence as we do disguising or acting as Captain Ahab. But they are existences only within a certain pattern of symbolic interpretation.

The same happens with other kinds of creative ideas, ones we might call inventions like cars, phones, rockets, electronic devices, etc. We always reshape existent matter according to different possibilities, and we cannot completely create or destroy existence. Therefore authors are only sub-creators, since the original creator can give whichever kind of reality, while we are limited to two of them: possibilities and necessities. We are the lords of two realms, but we can only use existence in a derivative way.[5]

## 2.2 *Assent*

Complete gestures imply awareness or self-control.[6] We are aware of the complete gestures we are performing, and a big part of the distinction between incomplete and complete gestures often depends on awareness. As we know, completion of gesture is given by the dense blending of semiotic elements, and an author's awareness puts any element into gestures and decides its density. So, we can learn a gesture by repetition of performances, but it becomes ours (and describes our personal identity, as we will see in the next chapter) only when it involves awareness. An author's endorsement makes our habitual gestures more or less significant, more or less close to "completion." And as we have already seen, "author" is a term that defines whoever is knowingly endorsing the gesture.

But how can we understand awareness while clinging to a philosophical externalist method typical of pragmatism, one that cannot accept a priori belief in some metaphorical and obscure sort of inner power or "intuition"?[7] We can list the problem of endorsement as the issue of assent. What is assent? Here again we would do better to rely on Peirce's account. According to my previous studies,[8] assent has a psychological, semiotic, and ethical nature. Setting aside the psychological part in which I am no expert – and I hope someone will carry out this task – I will focus on the semiotic aspect in this section, and on the normative level in the next one.

What is assent or acceptance from a purely semiotic point of view? Here again Peirce's insight can be useful. The semiotic aspect of "assent" coincides with the interpretant, the semiotic function that describes what comprehension is. What does it mean to be an interpretant? The interpretant is the outcome of the sign in a determination of the interpreter's mind (including all non-human minds). "Assent occurs when an interpretant gets expressed following the appeal made to it by a sign for the sake of an object. The object caused a question to be formulated, and, if it was expressed so as not to fall on deaf ears, at some point an answer or the beginning of one might get heard. When an interpretant lets itself be determined by a sign in the same respect in which the object determined that sign, the emergence of that interpretant indicates that the sign that appealed to it was assented to. A conclusion is an interpretant that assents to the argument offered in the premises" (De Tienne 2009).

Peirce was not satisfied with a simple definition and hence split up different kinds of interpretants, identifying the immediate interpretant with a "sense of comprehending the meaning of a sign," the dynamic interpretant with "a sense of effort," and the final or logical intepretant with a "habit of action" (*EP2*, 409). Even though Peirce understands the first interpretant as "apprehension" (ibid., 410), it is the dynamic interpretant that can actualize the possibility of that "apprehension" by either validating the representation or denying it (Peirce 1977, 111). From a semiotic point of view, then, assent is part of the work of the interpretant, and it is the condition through which our complete gesture becomes operatively meaningful. We have to endorse the representations through our acceptance and through our actual validation – that is, through our "yes" to the blending of representation that is about to happen.

This is a very important point of our creative process, and it is indeed the point of union between author and interpreter. The dynamic interpretant that implies assent happens for both author and interpreter, and it is a semiotic operation that both have to synthetically perform. Once again, this semiotic description vindicates Dewey's insight about the breadth of aesthetic experience and its radical refusal of any subject/object partition (1934, 54).

So we can explain the infinite possibility of re-performance of creative gestures that are never exactly the same. And we can also give account of the real activity that spectators perform. The spectator intervenes because his/her "yes" is required exactly like the author's, and the same holds for any kind of "complete (meaningful) gesture." In love, religion, education, science, and work – as in any other part of our lives – complete gestures require assent, and assent is a responsibility belonging to both author and interpreter. In the moment of assent they find their unity.

When we realize that creativity becomes effective only through assent, we feel diminished; our participation seems to amount to a small thing. But it illustrates the realist version of what Peirce was saying about being "in thought" and not, vice versa, owning our thought (*EP1*, 42). Our creative complete gestures always present only slight differences from contexts, habits, and gestures that precede them. Creation is never "out of the blue," and consists mainly in accepting what reality permits. Certainly, as we are going to see in the next section, creative acceptance also involves a re-formulation of aesthetic horizon. But for now it is important to establish that our creation is a personal endorsement of the reality to which we belong.

Notwithstanding its poverty, this explanation already accounts for two important features of our creative experience. On the one hand it explains why there is no creativity without the assumption of a tradition[9]; on the other hand it also accounts for the springing of creativity strictly understood from specific occasions. Creative gestures stem always from circumstances that can appear trivial to many, but are significant to the person who accepts them knowingly as a chance for meaning or as a responsibility. It is not a coincidence that "responsibility" comes from "respondeo" meaning "to answer." Creativity is our answer to the appeal of experience.

### 2.3 *Normative Appeal*

Responsibility means that assent also involves an ethical dimension. As we have seen, having to answer "yes" or "no" is part of the semiotic process. Signs require our participation, and any participation without our "yes" is a dissent, a formal repetition, or the heavy burden of an unexpressive routine. The responsibility we are talking about here is at a gnoseological level.[10] We have to judge whether the blending that is somehow proposed to us (whether we are authors or interpreters) is bad or good, or whether or not it is a "plausible" one, as Peirce would have said (*EP2*, 441).

What does "plausible" mean? We say that a hypothesis might be possible but it is not plausible, or that a character in a novel or in a movie is not verisimilar, namely it is not plausible. Sometimes we can even translate plausible as "reasonable" (ibid., 218). In any case, when we say "it is not plausible" we mean that it is of course possible – the idea belongs to the realm of possibilities – but it is not convenient to realize it. This inconvenience can be caused by various factors, such as economic ones, but the root of the inconvenience is generally that the proposal lies outside the range of effective possibilities. We can certainly be wrong in this judgment, and we usually rely only on the range of possibilities we have already accepted. A creative person is the one who expands this range. Florentine citizens, back in the fourteenth century, built the church of Santa Maria Novella without a dome. They thought of it but they did not have technical instruments to do the job. However, they thought that if it had been plausible, someone would have found the correct instrument. They were right, as Brunelleschi showed one hundred years later building up the dome.

The ethical statement is thus what Peirce would have called a secondness, something that has to deal with the effective world. Logically, we can say "yes" or "no" to a certain representation, but we need a broader judgment for understanding whether that particular complete gesture is worthwhile, and it is a judgment that involves the relationship of that gesture to the realm of existence. Ethics enters our reasoning by gestures assenting or dissenting to our proposed representation.

In Peirce's reconstruction, which I will endorse here, ethics enters the stage when we have to decide whether our reasoning is "good" or "bad."[11] It is obviously an ethical judgment even though it concerns reasoning since for Peirce reasoning is a habit of action and, like any habit, it can be ethically judged.

> Thus, logic is coeval with reasoning. Whoever reasons *ipso facto* virtually holds a logical doctrine, his *logica utens*. This classification is not a mere qualification of the argument. It essentially involves *an approval* of it, – *a qualitative approval.* Now such self-approval supposes self-control. Not that we regard our approval as *itself* a voluntary act, but that we hold the act of inference which we approve to be voluntary. That is, if we did not approve, we should not infer … But when we institute an experiment to test a theory, or when we imagine an extra line to be inserted in a geometrical diagram in order to determine a question in geometry, these are *voluntary acts* which our logic, whether it be of the natural or the scientific sort, *approves*. Now, *the approval of a voluntary act* is a *moral* approval. *Ethics is the study of what ends of action we are deliberately prepared to adopt.* (Ibid., 200)

"Ethics is the study of what ends of action we are deliberately prepared to adopt." This means that self-controlled actions begin only with the "qualitative approval" that puts the semiotic flux under self-control. Therefore, without ethical judgment there are no logical inferences, only mental acts.

Two *nota bene* are due at this point. The first one concerns the concept of "pure" and the second one the nature of self-control. "Ethics" is pure and not applied when it does not have any positive content, as Kant taught in a different sense. The content of ethics is the approval itself. In another image Peirce takes self-control as the gate at which perception enters our logical thought and the one from which purposive action takes its leave after reasoning (*CP* 5.212). Ethics is pure insofar as it has to intervene in any reasoning, whatsoever content it displays. It is a normative kind of judgment because it "distinguishes what ought to be from what ought not to be" (*EP*, 259). The characteristic of ethical judgment is to judge upon the conformity of actions to the ends that the person is deliberately prepared to adopt. In order to distinguish this normative role of ethics, Peirce even proposes to call it "antethics" (*EP2*, 377) and explains that its study illuminates the nature of the *summum bonum*. Besides, ethics cannot be confounded with the mere application of some maxim whose conformity is unavoidably judged with respect to the approved social order of the present epoch.

The second *nota bene* is about the nature of self-control. Peirce explicitly says that he does not "regard our approval as itself a voluntary act." The voluntary act is the act of inference that results from the approval. So what is the nature of this approval? It is this question that leads us to a final stretch of Peirce's writings, to fine-tune some of Peirce's insights for use in our proposal of complete gestures. In order to understand the nature of self-control, we have first to look at the way in which the approval is allowed or denied. Peirce indicates that the conformity of an action (of thought) to an end implies the knowledge of the end. This knowledge is not to be found within ethics, but within the superior normative science: aesthetics. "On the other hand, an ultimate end of action *deliberately* adopted – that is to say, reasonably adopted – must be a state of things that *reasonably recommends itself in itself* aside from any ulterior consideration. It must be an *admirable ideal*, having the only kind of goodness that such an ideal *can* have, namely esthetic goodness. From this point of view the morally good appears as a particular species of the esthetically good" (ibid., 201). Here good and bad can be seen in the light of what is "admirable." This is the profound teleological understanding of aesthetic values that Peirce brought into his analysis and that we can find in our synthetic turn based on complete gestures. Our creative blending has a judge, which is the admirable ideal we want to convey. It is this ideal into which our complete gestures, like our analytic reasoning, have to fit and with which they cooperate to propose, to enhance, and to foster. Conformity to this order is a qualitative judgment.

The artist, the educator, and anyone involved in a work knows this: our complete gestures are worthwhile only if they fit this admirable order that – according to reflexivity – they embody and enhance. Of what would this admirable order consist? According to Peirce, this admirableness coincides with a unity that "must have a multitude of parts so related to one another as to impart a positive simple immediate quality to their totality" (*EP2*, 201). Understood in this way, there is no aesthetic badness and the only "moral evil is not to have an ultimate aim." Peirce then identifies this ultimate aim, immutable as an aim and consistent with human freedom, with "concrete reasonableness" (*CP* 5.3) – that is, with the development of human reason in its capacity to govern individual events or in its "embodiment" (*EP2*, 255). The "embodiment" that concrete reasonableness forecasts lets us see the apex of Peirce's doctrine, in which he possibly foresees what a complete synthetic pattern would be. It is not a hard task to understand Peirce's normative path in light of the description of complete gestures. When we perform a complete gesture, we embody a vague possibility that we receive into a determinate action with a meaningful purpose. The purpose will emerge in the gesture as part of it. The blending of these three phenomenological/logical modalities and the kinds of signs that they display requires (also) an ethical statement. The "yes" or "no" to the creation of the complete gesture is pronounced according to the final admirable end that we want to understand/communicate/pursue; in the synthetic pattern, those ends or aims accompany one another in the same complete gesture.

We can understand concrete reasonableness as the order that any sort of reality must have to be comprehended. Complete gestures help to grow concrete reasonableness in any field. They do so by a performance that involves new particulars and that happens according to a specific law of interpretation. Therefore, there are as many orders as there are activities to which we are committed. In Peirce's terms we would say that there are different continua, or rather different aspects of the evolving continuum of reality. But obviously activities are connected to one another so that they form a "perfect" continuum of reality. Our complete gestures are following the admirable ideal to the extent that they help any particular to achieve the meaning of its own continuum of tradition and purpose. But the real aim of any complete gesture is to push any particular to fit, and thereby to help grow reality as such, passing from embodiment to embodiment, which are the different steps of our synthetic comprehension of reality. Pragmatically speaking this development means a progressive approach to a final recognition, to the "truth" understood as the result of inquiry in the long run (*EP1*, 139).

The ethical judgment that certifies the beginning of the self-controlled path of reasoning arises as an answer to a positive question proposed by nature or reality. Therefore, the final picture of the ethical judgment is this: it is an answer to the question that the continuity of reality proposes. This answer has a semiotic character (dynamic interpretant) but also an ethical one that is given by the "plausibility" of what reality proposes, according to the general, teleological, and aesthetical reasonableness.

# 6

# Figural and Narrative Identity

From this chapter on I will try to derive solutions to classic theoretical topics from the complete synthetic pattern and its main tool: the complete gesture. In the meantime, I hope that by demonstrating the application of this tool to different fields, I can help to clarify its task and properties. What personal identity actually is, and how we can recognize it, remain some of the most challenging topics of philosophy. They are also privileged tools to better understand the synthetic pattern that I am presenting. In this chapter I want to propose a new approach to these topics drawn from the synthetic path developed so far, which deals intrinsically with identity. Here I will focus on the second question: how can we recognize personal identity? I hope that this will also cast a light on the ontological theme of the first question, but I will not address it in this book directly.[1] We already established that the theme of recognizing identity is at the core of the philosophy of complete gestures and how it arises from the semiotic study of EG. We have yet to indicate the kind of personal identity that stems from the syntheticity that we defined earlier and which we have seen at work through complete gestures. I will name "figural identity" the kind of identity we obtain from this synthetic process.

We have many clues that recognition, understood as an inference based on signs, presides over some of the most interesting experiences of our thought; in our everyday experience this recognition is at work in the way in which memory works, in trials based on circumstantial evidence, in medical diagnoses, and in moral certainties. Peirce suggested that a recognition of signs plays a fundamental role in abduction.[2] All of these processes find their justification in their capacity to identify objects that appear at different moments. Therefore it is a problem that concerns the recognition of diachronic identity, and along with classic pragmatists Peirce tried to give a good analysis of it. However, we saw that these interesting rational processes suggest an inquiry that leads to a completely synthetic pattern. Then, we discovered that this pattern supplements the analytic one, and that its definition implies also a redefinition of analysis and a third, vague pattern of reasoning. Finally, we have seen that the synthetic reasoning understood as recognition of identity through a change can be performed synthetically through complete gestures. Thus, the considerations that I present here will refer to personal identity, but they will illuminate the entire paradigm I introduced in chapter 4

The case of personal identity so far has been reduced to the memory criterion, either in its original Lockean formulation or in one of its contemporary reformulations (Q-remembering [Shoemaker 1984]; psychological continuity criterion [Lewis 1976; Nozick 1981; Parfit 1971]). Reformulations show that as much as the memory criterion is evident and accepted, it is not clear what memory should technically be. To use one of Peirce's words, the memory criterion is vague. This does not mean that it is false. On the contrary, its vagueness is rich with suggestions that indicate the direction of inquiry. Now, the synthetic path we took and the tool of complete gesture will provide a technical explanation of what "memory" is and how it works in the case of personal identity.

## 1. CONTINUITY OF NARRATION

The first characteristic of the recognition of personal identity based on the philosophy of gesture shows what the multidimensional continuum and the line of identity (which is another continuum) expressed in EG are in our experience. It is the feature that many attentive critics have already introduced – a historical and narrative identity, already described by Ricoeur, Charles Taylor, Alasdair

MacIntyre, Colapietro, and many others.[3] It is a feature that does not imply gestures per se, but will be greatly ameliorated by the use of the tool of complete gestures.

We recognize a person because she turns out to be included in, or to belong to, the same narration. To give an example, let us recall the common experience of the recognition of ourselves at different moments, or of literary or artistic characters. We can also think of a scientific discovery in which an object that had already been explained is incorporated into a new theory, so that finally it is correctly interpreted and solves problems that the previous theory was not able to solve. But at this point in our discourse we can also think of some normal judgment such as "this body is heavy." They are always the same person/characters/object, but their determination has changed, whether because of autonomous mutation or because of their insertion into different explicative contexts. The problem of identity amounts to explaining this "sameness" and "difference" at the same time. It is our usual problem of the original model of synthesis as A=B. As anticipated, I will call "figures" the two different determinations at two different moments and I will use the case of a person as an example of how they work. The name *figura* will help us in what follows, establishing the different dynamic that I want to bring into the open. The passage or change between the two figures of the same/identical person taken at two different moments is the main point to which a synthetic reasoning on identity has to refer.

The first characteristic regards logic in a technical sense: returning to a term that I have already explained, the principle that regulates narrative identity is that of "true mathematical continuity," as Peirce used to call it.[4] This principle, if not interpreted according to the logic of set theory, holds that what is continuous is such in virtue of an essential regularity among realizations of possible states of things. Continuity is not a sum of very cohesive events. Peirce's later view exemplifies continuity through the image of time. Time precedes instances: there are instances because there is time, and no collections of instances can give us the continuity of time (*CP* 4.642). The cohesiveness that time represents is ontologically a possibility and, therefore, also the condition for any realization. But it is a condition that can be actualized only according to a general law of sequence. According to Peirce, continuity really means this passage from possibilities to realizations that become more and more necessary. In turn, we cannot understand time without these realizations.

What is this "true continuity" composed of? The instants of time may or may not be, but then they become actual realizations in experiences that happen in a sequence – in an order, which makes them necessary – and their being reveals what continuity is. Beyond the image of time, which is an aspect of a broader conception of "change," we can say that "true continuity" or "change" are Being in its perpetual transition through the three modalities of possibility, actuality, and necessity. Technically, here we can see the characteristics of a Peircean continuum: generality, modality, transitivity, reflexivity. Now, we have seen that complete gesture is the tool that embodies the synthetic path that Peirce discovered in EG. They are our meaningful habits of reasoning in action. Here I will take them as the basic elements that form the continuity of our personal identity.

In EG personal identity is continuity within continuity, the continuity established by the line of identity within the continuity of the plastic continuum of multiple dimensions. While explaining his gamma graphs, Peirce could maintain that a multidimensional plastic continuum can represent time and that a continuous line should represent identity on it.[5] Identity on this continuous surface means the continuity of one (possible) aspect at two different moments. If we translate this representation into a narration made of gestures within the narration of change, personal identity is a pure potentiality that becomes generality (necessity) through a singular act, sustained by the relationship with a narrative path. Being both continua, identity and narration have the same inner regularity – the same nature – that we already defined as transition through ontological modalities: a transition among the three modalities with a general tendency that goes from possibility to necessity. Narrativity is not, therefore, a moral problem but a logical function, although the term "logic" must be conceived in Peirce's broad semiotic way.

Such cohesiveness of change (the story) precedes the single analytic elements and thus is not the sum of them, just as "true continuity" does not coincide with the infinite piling of progressively greater sets. Narrativity precedes personal identity, continuity precedes division, and a synthetic pattern of reasoning precedes the analytic one in our knowledge of reality, thus respecting the experiential assumption from which pragmatism took its first steps. If we translate the idea of continuity into existential terms, that translation reveals that if one states that personal identity relies on a continuity it amounts to stating that personal identity belongs to a narrative pattern defined by the word "change." Certainly, this narrative pattern has often a temporal character, but the case of personal identity shows that we can have different continua. For one can recognize his/her identity as it belongs to different realizations of various changing continua: we can see and recognize personal identity through the continua of time, space, history, physical constitution, religion, love, etc. What is really important is that one has to belong to some narrative path in order to be understandable to others and to oneself.[6] A Peirce-driven understanding of continuity really is an improvement on some narrative patterns because we can precisely grasp the mathematical and logical core of identity.

As for "recognizing" an identity in a narrative pattern, Paul Ricoeur proposed a moral way (to keep promises), and Alasdair MacIntyre an epistemic-sociological way (to belong to a tradition of inquiry). Here I will articulate that identity through change is using complete gestures as an epistemic tool, as we derived it from the study of the line of identity in EG. So, if we want to look at how this logic for identity operates in our everyday experience, we can use the tool of complete gesture that has the same property of the line of identity in EG. We recognize identity in our everyday life through complete gestures, actions with a beginning and an end that bear a progressively determined meaning according to certain phenomenological and semiotic characteristics. These complete gestures have the same properties of the line of identity.

A couple of literary examples will help to clarify what complete gestures are in the case of personal identity. I will make use of these examples because they are extreme; in extremities we understand better what happens in everyday cases. Homer's Ulysses is recognized after twenty years when he strings the bow that will respond only to its master (Od. XXI, vv. 318–525). The moment is unlike any other moment during the days he spent, unknown to anyone, in Ithaca. It is a unique action, a gesture, that establishes a continuity between the person he was and the person he is after such a long passage of time. The gesture is complete because it represents an iconic quality (the kind of power the impossible stringing requires), an indexical actuality (the stringing itself as sign of the owner of the bow), a symbolic impact (return home and revenge, according to a teleology that I will explore in the next section). Phenomenologically speaking, it is an idea (power, which is a firstness) that becomes a fact (relation Ulysses-bow, which is a secondness), in order to develop a habit of action (relationship power-Ulysses-destiny of Ithaca, home, Penelope, etc.).

Another example is Jesus in the Gospel (Lc. 24, 13–35).[7] Jesus appears to two disciples and walks with them along the road. As the three men journey into the city of Emmaus, the two disciples have some emotional insight about Jesus' identity. But only when He breaks the bread do the two recognize Him. The reader understands that they could not recognize Him before because His aspect was different. However, in the complete gesture of breaking the bread, the new aspect revealed itself as identity (A=B in our previous terms) making them synthetize a new meaning – the Resurrection. Here again we find all of the phenomenological and semiotic requirements: the symbolic meaning (Resurrection) passes through the actual breaking of the bread as an index of His human/divine personality that the new and the old aspect have to show (icons). The relationship between Jesus, the disciples, and the surprising resurrection (thirdness) passes through the relationship between Jesus' hands and the bread he blesses (secondness) in order to express Jesus' human/divine nature (firstness).

These literary cases illustrate our usual way of reasoning about diachronic identity. Does not our memory function in the same way, even with ourselves? We do not recall a complete narration made of every single moment we have lived. We remember certain actions as significant to establishing the continuity of our identity. Those moments were the complete gestures that determined our identity. The continuity of narration is not given by the indissolubility of the chain of events, but instead by the antecedent pattern of sequence that makes singular spots continuous. As dots on a blackboard, which are continuous in virtue of their being similar forms belonging to the blackboard, complete gestures are similar events happening on the continuity of change as realization of possibilities that suggest a certain interpretation.

## 2. TELEOLOGY

In the second place, the continuity of personal identity that we are trying to delineate must have an aim – one that is, at least potentially, final. There are several logical and ethical reasons for that in the usual analytic pattern. First, we already know the semiotic teleology involved in symbols and in any semiosis as the source of communication.[8] But teleology is also proved in "critical logic" – the analytic study of the kinds of reasoning – by the logic of abduction. Abduction testifies that at least part of logic strictly understood relies upon teleology and looks for a synthetic pattern. In abduction we understand surprising phenomena as signs of an order or of an "essential" more comprehensive continuity, and the path of that understanding starts from the consequent in order to arrive at the antecedent.[9] Here we can pass from the consequent to the antecedent because of the continuity of the general "system of signs" (*EP2*, 494) and because of the identity of an object or person through those passages. Once again, we have here a continuity within a more general continuity, but the path of continuity that abduction shows also has a direction. As we know, the movement of abduction is backward (retroduction), and it can be backward because of the proleptic, or forward, aspect of reasoning as explained by the pragmatic maxim. Here again our inference is explained in terms of final causation: we can abduct something because the step "backward" (retro) would yield an understanding of the final result of our research. There is the passage from consequent to antecedent because there are consequent and antecedent, and because the consequent had already taken place. From this standpoint one of Peirce's merits is to have understood that the abductive pattern has to include something that is happening. He placed this surprising phenomenon at the beginning of his definition of abduction from 1903 on (ibid., 231).[10] This broad view of reality and teleology entering and determining logic is one of the reasons why the abductive pattern is so difficult to grasp for logicians. However, it is also the most evident clue of Peirce's rational feeling and drive for a synthetic pattern of reasoning that includes teleology as one of its characteristics. If our identity is a narrative, and it is continuity within continuity, it must respect teleology as an unavoidable element of the semiotic and logical pattern.

The second important reason for the teleological understanding of the continuity of narration is ethical. Ricoeur (1992) already pointed out this step very clearly when he proposed an ethically based fulfillment of *ipseitas* (identity). We know that someone is the same because she fulfills the aim she proposed, namely the promise she made. Without this kind of continuity directed toward an aim any narration would be difficult, and any kind of responsibility extremely problematic (i.e. any trial would become pointless). This commitment, which promises require and show, can also apply to any kind of fulfillment of practices, and these latter can even determine an entire tradition, as Macintyre suggested (1981). I fully agree with this moral consideration, and I find it more convincing if we also comprehend it within the pattern of a teleologically oriented continuity within the continuity of change. The figural or personal identity we are looking for will be therefore characterized by a narrative pattern, and so understood with a clear, intrinsic evaluative criterion.

Returning to our synthetic pattern, teleology is confirmed by the fact that complete gestures embody a direction and an aim. Identity today is a sign of the ultimate identity, just as what we believe today is, pragmatistically speaking, a sign of the ultimate truth (Maddalena 2010). Ulysses' or Jesus' gestures are signs of a final horizon that they want to reach or express. Personal identity was a vague possibility of some ideas, characteristics, aspects, and feelings, but as time goes by, it tends to become a general habit of action.

Are we not building our own identity through our complete gestures? Identity is more and more defined by what we have meaningfully done, and the more the identity is clear, the more it determines the future. Identity moves on a continuous reality composed by different modalities. The transition among possibility, existence, and necessity – the three modalities of reality – is essential to both reasoning and personality. We think of possibilities embodied in existent conditions and in general aims, and vice versa, our aims become more and more general according to actions performed on the basis of possible patterns. Does this mean that we pre-determine our future and that we are less and less free? Are habits like a straitjacket into which we have to shrink a little more each time, until a complete entropic determination opens up our pre-determined fate?[11] We have to answer this objection on two different levels. At an epistemological level, teleology is not pre-determination, but it is semiotically embodied in every gesture. Gestures have to be seen not as the outcome of what precedes us, but as prophecies or anticipations of the totality of meaning that we freely decide. Moreover they involve a decision, an assent from a semiotic, an ethical, and a psychological point of view. They involve a response to elements that we receive from reality. And we are not compelled to decide to use these elements in a gesture. So that, even though we are influenced largely by our antecedents – above all by our antecedent gestures – we are always free to answer in a different way. In EG Peirce represented this situation as well: the line of identity on a multidimensional continuum has to become a line of teridentity, namely a couple of lines that have the same beginning but two different ends, one of which does not abut to an actual point. This "loose end" shows that there are possibilities that have the same origin but have not been (or have not yet been) realized (*CP* 4.583).[12] Moreover, the completion of gesture implies an always-new deepening of the iconic level that represents the object of experience as far as its form is concerned. Therefore, there is no complete gesture without a revision of initial possibilities that can always end up with different outcomes. Sure enough, previous performances highly influence the actual performance. However, the structure of a complete gesture contains this renewal of possibilities that differentiates it from repetitions.

The objection has a second level. Are we defending a sort of ontological pre-determination? Is the series of our gestures leading us unavoidably to an end? For the first question, the answer relies on the conception of continuity. The kind of continuity we described as "true" or "real" means that we do not have to follow an uninterrupted series, so that we do not have to build our identity through the coherence of our gestures. As existence plainly shows, coherence helps identification, but continuity is something more profound, of which coherence is only a specific case. To stick with gestures, it is their meaningfulness or their "completion" that decides how important they are for identity, so that we can rebuild our true identity, connecting something that happens today to a gesture we learned years ago. Many kinds of "conversions" are really cases of conjunction with something meaningful and forgotten that happened in the past. Since complete gestures imply a logic of modalities based on transition, the general direction toward full determination does not forbid a swinging back to possibilities. It implies only that you cannot reset previous embodiments completely. But you can still say that continuity is ontological – if not moral – pre-determination. Here lies the metaphysical core of the conception of gesture as a synthetic tool that I will try to develop: reality develops through gestures, and it implies the a posteriori foundation that Peirce found as a property of mathematics. Our gestures cooperate with this development, so that what we do through gestures becomes part of reality. However, setting aside this ontological issue, our account of narrative continuity is only a semiotic and logical (not metaphorical) explanation of the narrativity well acknowledged by critics in the last forty years.

Now, we have to see how this "building up" or, conversely, this "recognition" of personal identity happens. I will state here only the recognition part that is easier to express, because it requires fewer new logical tools. But the dramatic piling up and development of complete gestures could be easily imagined as the other side of what I am proposing.

## 3. "FIGURALITY" FROM "FIGURA," WHICH MEANS "PERSON." A NEW WAY TO LOOK AT IDENTITY AND MEMORY

I have maintained that recognizing an identity is not only a matter of continuity, which is the necessary ground, or of teleology, which points out the direction of continuity. "Recognizing" is also a precise path (in EG representation it is the drawing of the line of identity) within that continuity (the multidimensional continuum of assertion). This path has a semiotic and phenomenological pattern that, as we have seen, consists in the dense blending of icons, indices, and symbols (and firstness, secondness, and thirdness). This dense blending guarantees the continuity of identity itself in the transition from vague possibility to actual realizations, and to necessary future conditionals. When we tried to understand how this complex pattern works, we realized that we embody this kind of reasoning in complete gestures that include all the characteristics that analysis found.

Complete gestures as the embodied way to represent or recognize identity are different from the two main representations of identity: identity as permanence of attributes and identity as dialectic.[13] The kind of identity that stems from our discourse on complete gestures is a development of experience. We have said that identity is recognized through complete gestures, and that this recognition coincides with complete gestures themselves. Identity and recognizing an identity through change are one and the same phenomenological and semiotic determined action. In a synthetic pattern, re-cognition is an action and not a conceptual or mental analysis.[14]

But how do complete gestures connect to one another? Here the idea of figure becomes relevant and moves a step beyond EG, which remain a very powerful analysis of our synthetic reasoning, but which cannot achieve a complete synthesis of reasoning and method of inquiry. Erich Auerbach, the great Dante scholar, proposed a theory of figura and I would like to briefly point out how it is implemented within our conception of complete gestures. According to Auerbach: "'figura' is something real and historical which announces something else that is also real and historical. The relation between the two events is revealed by an accord or similarity" (1959, 29). Moreover "figural interpretation establishes a connection between two events or persons, the first of which signifies not only itself but also the second, while the second encompasses or fulfills the first. The two poles of the figure are separate in time, but both, being real events or figures, are within time, within the stream of historical facts" (ibid., 53). Dante's figures in the heavenly kingdom have a definitive, or final, meaning: they are saved in Paradise, penitent but still saved in Purgatory, and damned in Hell. Dante's characters have already reached the knowledge of their final destiny, the end of inquiry, the final individual meaning. What is the relationship between these figures and their antecedents on earth? How can Dante, the heavenly pilgrim, recognize friends and foes? He recognizes them because they are readable within the same figural interpretation, notwithstanding their being two different objects at two different moments of time. The relationship between the two figures has a physical, moral, and ontological antecedent on earth, and a physical, moral, and ontological consequent in heaven. So there is an order, and a teleology, of the "sequence." However, Dante's (and our) understanding of those characters travels both ways, remembering (memory) and anticipating (forecasting). Ulysses remembers his fascinating tragic death from the depth of the Inferno (Inf., XXVI, vv. 49–142). In Canto V of Purgatory, Bonconte da Montefeltro tells of the end of his life, explaining as his last word – the name of the Virgin – opened up the road to salvation (Pur., V, vv. 94–129). In the tale he anticipates the end that Dante is seeing before his eyes.

Even more significant for understanding the idea of figure is what Cato represents. The great Roman politician is suicidal and a friend of Caesar's murderers. However, Dante, who thought so highly of Caesar and the Roman Empire, sets Cato as the guardian of Purgatory. On the penitents' beach Virgil shows us that Cato is the figure of freedom. Being a figure means that the historical Cato, who did not want to give up Rome to Caesar, was the pre-figuration of the freedom he himself, a heavenly historical character, is embodying in Heaven. Virgil even forecasts "the great day" in which Cato's body ("the cloth") "will shine so bright" (Pur., I, v. 75). In Cato we can see all the characteristics of figurality: the relationship between past and present, and the forecasting of a complete end. The complete end tells us that the process is ongoing and that it has a telos, a purpose; but it permits a logical/ontological movement between different modalities. "Figural prophecy implies the interpretation of one worldly event through another; the first signifies the second, the second fulfills the first. Both remain historical events; yet both, looked at in this way, have something provisional and incomplete about them; they point to one another and both point to something in the future, something still to come, which will be the actual, real and definitive" (Auerbach 1959, 58). Auerbach's *figurae* have all of the phenomenological and semiotic characteristics that we detected in complete gestures. They represent a general meaning in one action, in which they synthetize the possible aspects of a person. Auerbach did not have the tools necessary to understand the powerful synthetic logic that *figurae* use and show. Moreover, he was not aware of how figurae could help us comprehend our usual way of reasoning. But the theoretical path we have walked so far permits us to know it better. In fact, the heavenly figure is always tied with the earthly one. What is this bind that links them together? Auerbach defines the bind only with the word "similarity." But now we can know similarity better, thanks to the idea of complete gestures. In our conception of synthetic reasoning, the recognition of identity through change happens because of the complex reading of signs involved in complete gestures.

Auerbach tries to sever figural interpretation both from myth and allegory. But his amazing historical and philological analysis falls short of a proper "speculative grammar." Peirce's tools show us that myths and allegories function at a symbolic level, which can hardly explain the radical mixture of history and meaning that we find in figures. As we know from our study of complete gestures, the burden of signification falls not only upon symbols, but also equally upon indices and icons. The form of the object – the figura of figura – appears at an iconic level, and its actualization happens always at an indexical level. Proper names and pronouns, for example, are indexical tools in the linguistic realm.

Therefore, the theory of figurality and the tool of complete gesture supplement one another. On the one hand, the blending of phenomenological and semiotic levels leads to complete gestures, and they are indeed the way in which the recognition of identity between the two figures is triggered (or not triggered, in the case of vague judgments). Only the melded action of the three kinds of sign and the three kinds of phenomena can account for the recognition of personal identity. On the other hand, figurality explains the way in which complete gestures operate on one another. They form a continuity that is not an uninterrupted series of events. The connection is internal to complete gestures themselves. Because of the phenomenological and semiotic structure we have already studied, each gesture works as a figura of other previous and successive complete gestures. Therefore, each of them fulfills a previous complete gesture and signifies a future one, somehow always building up and prefiguring a final horizon: the truth, pragmatically understood (see *EP1*, 139).[15]

Is the figural identity pattern valid also in everyday cases of recognition? I think so. Dante's conception is only an extreme case that sets up the topic of recognition because it shows two different moments in two severed ontological realms, heaven and earth. Figural identity is the tool to pass from one to the other. But is not our identity always physically and morally different at two different moments in time? The cells in our bodies change, so that from year to year we are not the same. We have to fulfill plans, promises, contracts, etc. made at previous moments in time. The ontological discourse is obviously more complicated but displays similar issues. If we accept Peirce's understanding of modalities as the transitional structure of reality, we can certainly say that identity develops through possible ideas, which become actual realizations and necessary habits of action. Something that was only an idea is now a habit of action. One was not married, and now he is. Is he still the same person? Even more so, when we completely change the attitude of our life, as in famous cases of conversion (Saul the persecutor who becomes Paul the saint), are we still the same person? Complete gestures are the real continuity of identity. As we have seen, they simultaneously define our identity and allow for a transformation of it. Moreover, figurality among complete gestures seems to describe what happens with memory. We remember synthetic points of our experience. Complete gestures coincide with the points that define that particular case of identity A=B, which we call personal identity.

The ontological discourse deserves a more detailed study that is not part of this book. For now, it is sufficient to say that we can see these ontological differences between two figures at two different moments in our everyday lives, and complete gestures are the way in which we can knit them together. Our physical, moral, and ontological identity is not a pure, plain continuum; rather, it is continuity between complete gestures that have built, and continue to build, our identity so that we can recognize it. Even more, the building of our identity is propelled by a final yet vague end for which we hope, and about which we – rightly or wrongly – forecast. The relationship between the two figures establishes also a path of future realization, which will be another figure in our ongoing process. So we can explain why recognition of identity is always going on. Dante's "second figures" are in a definitive realm (except Purgatory, as in Cato's case) and we are not, but the dynamic of our development and of its recognition is the same. Sure enough, there must be a general continuity of change on which we scribe our life, and we belong to it. But our personality is a specific line that our complete gestures embody in leading toward a purpose. We are strongly influenced by the continuum – the tradition to which we belong – but we are not pre-determined by it. As with Dante's characters, a few complete gestures, and even only one, can be enough to say who we are.

# 7

# Writing as Complete Gesture:

## An Example of Complete Gesture

In this chapter I will follow the same strategy that I used with personal identity. On the one hand I will face a specific problem – artistic creativity – and apply the tool of complete gesture in order to verify whether this application will better fit research on this topic than do the currently available tools. On the other hand, this application will deepen the characteristics of complete gesture, broadening our view of this tool and of the synthetic pattern of knowledge to which it belongs.

With regard to applied creativity, J.R.R. Tolkien used to say that the entire saga of *The Hobbit* and *The Lord of the Rings* was born from writing the sentence, "in a hole in the ground there lived a hobbit," without knowing what a hobbit was going to be (Carpenter 1995, letter 63). The observation is far from trivial. Leonhard Euler maintained the same when he said that the entire power of his mathematics lived in his pencil (Vailati 2003, 87). Peirce's and Wittgenstein's notes on "doing mathematics" as the foundation of mathematics are similar to these statements (Chauviré 2008, 191–5). Many contemporary mathematicians seem to hold this perspective, accepting that the creative part of mathematics is made by gestures. As affirmed in chapter 5, the tool of complete gesture will provide a synthetic account of creativity. In this chapter, I want to propose a literary example in order to reach a double result. I want to show first that literature "naturally" relies on complete gestures as its usual way to represent and therefore comprehend experience. This preliminary result will confirm what has previously been said about complete gestures as a supplement to analytic reasoning.

Almost unwillingly this chapter also suggests a critical theory of literature. As a matter of fact, literature is presented here in terms of always being connected with comprehension and the communication of meaning. It would be easy to understand literature as a specific case of knowledge and, according to the density of the blending of signs, to judge examples of literature (and art) as more or less successful if two criteria are met: 1) if any knowledge is representation and any representation is constituted by semiosis and 2) if a complete gesture is a particular kind of semiosis constituted by different and densely arranged types of signs and phenomena.

Once again, pragmatism will vindicate common sense in accepting that works of art could be more or less appreciated. This attitude does not mean that those judgments are mandatory (by which authority?), but only that it is possible to look at artwork in a more precise way, trying to justify or correct our impressions through the appreciation of different elements present in the work itself. The philosophy of gesture does not want to focus on a theory of a certain field. It only wants to understand its own tool (complete gesture) better in order to understand the development of knowledge better. This chapter will present a specific translation of the semiotic and phenomenological elements of complete gestures into actions, grammatical and syntactical notions, and kinds of interpretation. The case is taken from literature. In this application, complete gestures show how they can help explain topics that are usually understood more vaguely. Further studies will deepen this inchoative inquiry, which for the time being serves the purpose of exemplary intention rather than exhaustiveness. Nevertheless in this attempt the tool of complete gesture reveals itself as a powerful instrument. With the use of this instrument new kinds of research may be born in many fields, even though this is not the aim of this book.

This chapter will rely on Peirce's semiotic, and on the example of Vasily Grossman as an author. It will show why and how writing is a synthetic tool of knowledge that we can call a gesture, and in doing so it will explain creativity in a pragmatist pattern. It will then explain why and how this gesture, when it is complete, fosters knowledge beyond any analysis, including an author's analytic knowledge of his creation.

## 1. SETTING UP A SCENE

Vasily Grossman is one of the twentieth century's most important but lesser-known masters of writing. Born in 1905, he grew up in a Jewish family and was completely immersed in communist, multicultural, and revolutionary ideas. At quite a young age he became a well-respected, integrated writer of the regime, thanks to Gorky's approval of his short stories (Garrard 2012). During the Second World War, Grossman became nationally famous. He lost his mother in the first Nazi attack. She was executed, as thousands of Jews had been, in the Grossman family's city, Berdichev (Ukraine). Feeling guilty for not having been quick enough to rescue his mother and to summon her to Moscow, Grossman enrolled in the Red Army, where he was soon chosen as a reporter for the Red Star, the newspaper of the Army. Following the troops, Grossman fought at Stalingrad where he did his work courageously while Nazi and Soviet armies clashed on the Right Bank (and party members fled to the safe Left Bank).

After the war Grossman started working on a big novel representing the Stalingrad Battle. The first part of the novel, *For a Just Cause*, was not published until 1952, and only Stalin's death stopped major and potentially very dangerous critiques that were appearing in official newspapers. Critiques were the result of the growing anti-Semitism of Stalin's regime, even though the novel was following the rhetorical truths and patterns of Soviet literature. In the 1950s Grossman worked on the second part of the novel, during which he changed his perspective. He decided to speak the truth at all costs. The cost was high. The manuscript of *Life and Fate* was seized by the KGB (1961) and Grossman's complaints to authorities remained unheard. Grossman died a few years later (1964), isolated from his friends and without the possibility of further publishing. A copy of his masterpiece was smuggled to Western countries in 1978, and later published in 1980 in Switzerland. Only in recent years has Grossman become popular.[1]

This brief biographical sketch is necessary to understand the first step of this chapter: writing is a complete gesture by which we come to know something in a synthetic way. In order to explain how a complete gesture works in this case, let us take a meaningful example from Grossman's *Life and Fate*. In a famous episode of the book, the commandant of a Nazi camp, Liss, summons an old Soviet prisoner, Mostovskoy. The latter is one of the first Bolsheviks, Lenin's comrade, and one of the main characters of the Revolution. Liss does not want to interrogate the old communist. He wants to force him to listen to his well-pondered theory about the absolute equivalence of the Nazi and Soviet systems. The scene starts as an interrogation, but reveals itself to be a strange sort of dialogue.

> "I've been summoned for interrogation," he [Mostovskoy] said out loud. "There's nothing for us to talk about." "Why do you say that?" asked Liss. "All you see is my uniform. But I wasn't born in it. The Führer and the Party command; the rank and file obey. I was always a theoretician. I'm a Party member, but my real interest lies in questions of history and philosophy. Surely not all the officers in your NKVD love the Lubyanka?" … "When we look one another in the face, we're neither of us just looking at a face we hate – no, we're gazing into a mirror. That's the tragedy of our age. Do you really not recognize yourselves in us – yourselves and the strength of your will? Isn't it true that for you too the world *is* your will? Is there anything that can make *you* waver?" (Grossman 2011, 378–9)

"We are gazing into a mirror" is Grossman's conclusion. Today this historical statement seems almost trivial, albeit not universally accepted. However, it was not trivial at all in 1961, when this similarity was rarely affirmed in the Western world, and never in the Soviet Union.[2] In Grossman's case literature represented an inconvenient truth: it showed this sad equivalence well before it was known to historians in its particulars and to philosophers in its reasons.

Literature wields a comprehending power through its representation. What is the dynamic of such a process of knowledge? How is it connected to creativity? In what sense is it a pragmatist's way to look at knowledge? In pragmatist terms, we could say that Grossman had *an* experience of this political reality (Dewey 1934,

42). He fought at Stalingrad and he saw the atrocities perpetrated by both armies. Even more, he realized how on that occasion, soldiers in both fields were caught up by ideologies through party control. As a matter of fact, Grossman's novel showed that soldiers from both sides became more human when they lost contact with their parties, which happened when they were losing the battle. Germans and Soviets experienced the same path of rescue from ideologies. When one has an experience like this, a powerful experience for which there is no previous pattern of understanding (at that time ideology was not considered and studied in all its mechanisms as it is now and it was hard to understand what was going on), the synthetic path of knowledge emerges more clearly than usual because we have to synthetize different and strange data. This path for understanding is constituted semiotically and phenomenologically, and this path forms a complete gesture.

How is complete gesture important for describing what is going on in a context such as Grossman's? An accomplished knowledge can be summarized by words, that is, at a symbolic level displaying an accomplished meaning that can be analyzed conceptually. New and difficult situations, like the Stalingrad battle and the clash of ideologies, were too powerful and too unknown to be already well-formed and ready for analysis. A communist writer was facing both the strength and the falsity of his native culture. His world was collapsing before him. In technical terms, experiences like this are vague and need comprehension. As we have seen, the processes of representing and comprehending are unified for pragmatists, so much so that any comprehension – that is, any semiosis – is somehow a creative process if we understand creativity in a broad sense. Grossman, like any artist, displays this ordinary semiotic pattern at a more visible level: he actually has to employ different levels of signs at the same time in order to represent (or comprehend) experience. He has to give an iconic-indexical-symbolic form to the object (the experience) he wants to represent. This "giving form" happens on both a phenomenological and a semiotic level. The action of representing is a complete gesture, through which he comprehends and communicates his particular experience. This form of performing representation goes well beyond what symbols may say.

On the phenomenological level the experience is an indeterminate form, what we call a "vague idea" in ordinary language. It is the level of firstness, of the idea in itself. The more the experience is relevant for a person, the more it is full of effects or meaning that cannot be clear and distinct immediately. When the author starts writing, it becomes effective (secondness) in the action of the actual scribing. Material or virtual writing modifies the idea, making it existent. This passage clarifies the initial vagueness, even though it impoverishes its abysmal depth. This is why we have the impression that the actual writing is the source of thought itself: the idea becomes clear in the very act of writing. Finally, a complete picture of the situation, with characters and dialogues, emerges *while* we are writing. The complete displaying of the form of experience is a thirdness, a relationship among experience and the signs of its interpretation. Thirdness is the new reality formed from both the initial experience and its phenomenological and semiotic development. It is a new form of reality, independent of what any thinker or even the majority of thinkers can understand or speak. The dialogue between Liss and Mostovskoy is a reality: it provokes effects and it is independent of any opinion.

On the semiotic level, the idea takes the shape of images, icons: images are the set-up of the scene in the camp and the actions that the characters perform from the initial description of Liss' physical aspect to the final movement with which Mostovskoy grasps the manuscript that Liss entrusts to him (Grossman 2011, 375–87). Proper names are indices, connecting characters and geophysical entities. Liss and Mostovskoy are obviously the first two proper names that render the situation alive, but there are many: Stalin, Hitler, NKVD, Lubyanka, etc. Nicknames or titles like "the Führer," "our chief," and so on are also indices. Finally, the discourse itself is a symbol that proceeds through words and that develops a meaning toward which the scene tends.

In a sense the semiotic analysis can be much more complicated. To be thorough it should say that icons and indices are expressed by symbols (words), so that we could talk of pure symbols, and/or degenerate symbols of different levels (that contain indices and icons, only indices, only icons, etc.). However, at this point I am not interested in this kind of analysis because I want only to cast a light on what happens in the representation of experience through writing.

As we know, once the semiotic and the phenomenological levels are blended in a dense way a particular action called complete gesture arises. In the dialogue between Liss and Mostovskoy, you can see the complete gesture at work and the comprehension of *an* experience that it affords, while it communicates its representation. The meaning of the mirror theory emerges within the complete articulation of gestures on the scene. The complete gesture of the scene is the embodiment of the sad mirroring of two totalitarianisms, and at the same time, they give birth to and enhance that same meaning.

## 2. MORE THAN THE AUTHOR

What does "dense blending" of signs mean in this case? What kind of knowledge does it permit? We already tried to answer these questions, but I am sure that another example taken from Grossman's masterpiece will provide new awareness of the implications and the conditions of complete gestures.

Grossman's main concept is the nature and the dynamic of freedom, as opposed to ideology. With Grossman, we find a theoretical explanation of what freedom is. Mostovskoy receives a manuscript from Liss that is written by Ikonnikov, a "fool of God" who is prisoner in the camp. In accordance with an ancient literary tradition, since he is considered a "fool" Ikonnikov is allowed to tell the truth (2011, part II, ch. 15). The truth is that any form of good is ideological. In the name of the good, so many atrocities have been committed; one would be blind not to notice that any theorization of the good becomes evil and violent. Moreover, through Ikonnikov, Grossman indicates that this evil is not only at a human level. Beasts and even trees fight one another in order to survive. Evil seems to cover the entire development of any living being, even though Grossman observes throughout the book that living in itself is the only good and the only meaning we can attribute to the words freedom and life. This double conviction is paradoxical: life is good and free; the development of life and its unavoidable death is evil and slavish (ibid., 539). Ikonnikov's solution is that the good is opposed to kindness. Kindness is the practical, illogical, small attitude that common people show to one another outside of any theoretical consideration.

These are Grossman's theoretical statements. Paradoxical as they are, the only way in which the author can express them is by representing them through gestures. And gestures must be complete in order to reach meaningfulness. Even in Ikonnikov's text this illogical goodness has to be shown by examples made of gestures, so much so that Ikonnikov's manuscript tells the story of the old Russian woman whose husband has just been shot by Nazi occupants. Eventually she will help the German soldier who is accidentally wounded at her apartment. How can it be so? It cannot be: there is no reason for her willingness to help. Illogical, silly, practical kindness: this is the only reflex of the original freedom of life.

> This senseless kindness is condemned in the fable about the pilgrim who warmed a snake in his bosom. It is the kindness that has mercy on a tarantula that has bitten a child. A mad, blind, kindness. People enjoy looking in stories and fables for examples of the danger of this senseless kindness. But one shouldn't be afraid of it. One might just as well be afraid of a freshwater fish carried out by chance into the salty ocean.
>
> The harm from time to time occasioned a society, class, race or State by this senseless kindness fades away in the light that emanates from those who are endowed with it.
>
> This kindness, this stupid kindness, is what is most truly human in a human being. It is what sets man apart, the highest achievement of his soul. No, it says, life is not evil!
>
> This kindness is both senseless and wordless. It is instinctive, blind. When Christianity clothed it in the teachings of the Church Fathers, it began to fade; its kernel became a husk. It remains potent only while it is dumb and senseless, hidden in the living darkness of the human heart. (Ibid., 393)

But this theoretical discourse with its internal examples is not Grossman's best representation of his experience. In another episode of the book, Sofya Osipovna is a Russian doctor. She is taken prisoner at Stalingrad. During the long journey by train, she becomes acquainted with a young orphan, David. The train takes them to Treblinka. Once off the train, she has the opportunity to escape the gas chamber by declaring her status as a doctor. However, she decides to stay with the child, who is already affectionate with her. Their painful journey terminates in the gas chamber. Here Grossman has to represent one of the crudest experiences of humanity. "Speech was no longer of any use to people, nor was action; action is directed towards the future and there no longer was any future" (ibid., 537). The symbolical level is declared here to be insufficient.

> Sofya Levinton felt the boy's body subside in her arms. Once again she had fallen behind him. In mine-shafts where the air becomes poisoned, it is always the little creatures, the birds and mice, that die first. This boy, with his slight, bird-like body, had left before her.
>
> 'I've become a mother,' she thought.
>
> That was her last thought.
>
> Her heart, however, still had life in it: it contracted, ached and felt pity for all of you, both living and dead; Sofya Osipovna felt a wave of nausea. She pressed David, now a doll, to herself; she became dead, a doll. (Ibid., 538)

Grossman's theoretical statements about kindness are presented through a complete gesture here. Taking for granted the phenomenological analysis of the gesture that any author has to perform if she is setting up a scene, let us concentrate on the semiotic level of the scene. Everything is described by words – symbols – but words are declared impotent at describing what is going on. Thus words have to work not at a conceptual level, but at an iconic and an indexical level. Indices are decisive here, in order to recapture what Sofya's and David's lives were. "Her eyes – which had read Homer, *Izvestia*, *Huckleberry Finn* and Mayne Reid, that had looked at good people and bad people, that had seen the geese in the green meadows of Kursk, the stars above the observatory at Pulkovo, the glitter of surgical steel, the *Mona Lisa* in the Louvre, tomatoes, and turnips in the bins at market, the blue water of Issyk-Kul – her eyes were no longer of any use to her. If someone had blinded her, she would have felt no sense of loss" (ibid., 537). David's memories are not strictly indexical, but by using a list, an indexical value emerges: common names are used as labels more than descriptions.[3] "He had taken only a few steps in the world. He had seen the prints of children's bare heels on hot, dusty earth, his mother lived in Moscow, the moon looked down and people's eyes looked up at it from below, a teapot was boiling on the gas-ring ... This world, where a chicken could run without its head, where there was milk in the morning and frogs he could get to dance by holding their front feet – this world still preoccupied him. All this time David was being clasped by strong warm hands. He didn't feel his eyes go dark, his heart become empty, his mind grow dull and blind. He had been killed; he no longer existed" (ibid., 538). The strong, last hug in which Sofya understands her motherhood is the iconic image that sums up the entire, ineffable feeling of that old lady for the young son of her people: the profound unity, the unutterable piety, the rage against the enemy, and the deep unanswered questions about the utility of her life. But that hug opens up the last (symbolic) thought: I've become a mother. From the ultimate border of the evil, the greatest answer to her eternal questions stems.

At a semiotic level, in this interlude between Sofya and David all three kinds of signs are present in a much more poignant and artistically convincing way than in the short description of the old Soviet woman and the Nazi soldier. We should say that the signs are densely blended. Cleverly, symbols as such (words) are proclaimed to be silent in a scene of death. However, the scene is described through words and, at the end, it is a word that expresses a well-formed thought about being a mother, the real meaning of the story that has been fostered by the complete gesture as a whole. Indices are used to recapture existence, playing on their power to label existent experiences. Icons describe the movements in the gas chamber: those movements represent the emptiness of insensate death, as well as the deep meaning of that last hug. Everything holds together in a proportion that we could judge as dense, namely able to perform a complete gesture.

Now, let us go back to our questions: what does a dense blending of signs mean? What kind of knowledge does it permit? We saw that "dense blending" means that this action has elements of originality. It represents the forms of the experience from which it stems (iconic level); it has an actual determination in existence (index); it has a scope (symbol), a final destination that is the ideal end that the single realization has to confirm, and that will verify the goodness or the plausibility of the act itself.

In Ikonnikov's manuscript, the icons are so weak that we encounter the typical tone of theoretical statements. They are still creative in a way, since they are forms of artistic writing as well, but they lack the power and the novelty with which icons describe the process of understanding within an experience. Theory is already settled; art becomes repetition, although in a noble sense. Indices grant us connection with hard existence. If we imagined Sofya's scene without indices, we would not understand the richness of the persons we are losing in the gas chamber because the lists of memories make us comprehend who they were. Without indices the story would become a model, losing that full embodiment in particulars that is the core of synthetic reasoning understood in a synthetic pattern. Without symbols, the final revelation of the episode would be lost and Sofya's death would only remain a monstrosity. In technical terms, it would remain information without meaning.

From these semiotic characteristics, the answer to the second question arises. What kind of knowledge does complete gesture permit? When a gesture is complete we understand something more in a determinate way. Any synthesis brings us something new, but this kind of synthesis clarifies in one act an entire idea or concept. Sometimes, as in this passage, we understand something more than the author himself/herself. In the chapter following Sofya's death (ibid. II, 49), Grossman explains his philosophy again. He underlines that when a person dies, an entire universe that she had in herself dies. Only in human existence does life become happiness, freedom, supreme value. Death is slavery. "When a person dies, they cross over from the realm of freedom to the realm of slavery. Life is freedom, and dying is a gradual denial of freedom" (ibid., 539). However, Sofya's episode has just shown something more: death is an opportunity for supreme humanity.

In many other passages, Grossman shows this unique quality of the complete gestures that he creates, so much so that when the scene is ended, often questions and not theories arise. When the colonel Darensky defends a mistreated German soldier against a Soviet general, he does not preach about justice. He asks himself questions about his relationship with his people and his nature. "What an abyss lay between the road he was following today and the road he had taken to Yashkul through the Kalmyk steppe. Was he really the same man who, beneath an enormous moon, had stood on what seemed to be the last corner of Russian earth? Who had watched the fleeing soldiers and the snake-like necks of the camels, tenderly making room in his heart for the poor, for the weak, for everyone whom he loved?" (ibid., 698). The thousands of questions that fill up *Life and Fate* show that the last answer to the problem of the nature of life and freedom is not the theory of Ikonnikov's manuscript, but a much more complicated paradox: life is good at its origin and it is free; death is evil and is pursued by nature as well as by human beings. But death and evil cannot be a nihilist final description for there is something more in life, something good that makes us raise questions about the meaning of life, even when evil seems to triumph. It is the meaning of the fertile death of Sofya Levinton. The human in humanity is not only senseless kindness, but a rational link with the meaning of the universe. This link is usually expressed by small and big questions, such as those that Alexandra Vladimirovna asks at the end of the book.

> The lives of those close to her were unsettled, confused, full of doubts and mistakes, full of grief. What would happen to Lyudmila? What would be the outcome of her family troubles? Where was Seryozha? Was he even alive? How hard things were for Viktor Shtrum! What would happen to Vera and Stepan Fyodorovich? Would Stepan be able to rebuild his life again and find peace? ... And Vera? ... And Zhenya? Would she follow Krymov to Siberia? ... Why were their destinies so confused, so obscure? ... No, whatever life holds in store – hard-won glory, poverty and despair, or death in a labour camp – they will live as human beings and die as human beings, the same as those who have already perished; and in this alone lies man's eternal and bitter victory over all the grandiose and inhuman forces that ever have been or will be. (Ibid., 846)

Complete gestures illustrate this triple enigma of good, evil, and meaningfulness much more than Grossman's theory, which reaches only the first two steps without any other philosophical solution.

The dense blending of signs typical of complete gestures displays the way in which creativity grasps the too-complicated experience of reality. When gestures are not complete, they are more ordinary; they represent less and they understand less. However, as we have seen, they are always partly creative, insofar as they provide new synthetic knowledge. In the distinction that I made in chapter 4 between completeness and incompleteness of gesture we can see the difference between ordinary and extraordinary creativity in life, science, and arts. When creativity is extraordinary, the complete gesture grasps experience more than the author himself/herself is aware of. In these cases, the gesture becomes an independent reality, a common property of author and reader in the assent they have to give.[4]

## 3. LITERARY SELF-REFLECTION UPON CREATIVITY

The philosophy of complete gestures, when utilized as a key to comprehending what creativity is, respects all pragmatist insights. Its foundation lies in the recognition of a deep continuity between reality, representation, and interpretation, as all pragmatists have advocated. A final example taken from Grossman will show how much this picture of creativity embedded in experience is a common attribute of all those who reflect or try to represent their own creativity. In *Life and Fate* the scientist Shtrum, Grossman's alter ego, discovers the conception of the new nuclear power. In that moment Grossman describes how creativity works. Here again the representation is superior to the author's ideas. Grossman wants to say that – contrary to Marxism – ideas are not the product of practice, but in the description of it he affirms a much more profound unity between the whole experience and comprehension. In this necessarily long description, the phenomenological path of ideas in themselves (firstness), physical actions (secondness), and final destination appears (thirdness).

> And at the same time his head had been full of other laws and relationships: quantum interactions, fields of force, the constants that determined the processes undergone by nuclei, the movement of light, and the expansion and contraction of space and time. To a theoretical physicist the processes of the real world were only a reflection of laws that had been born in the desert of mathematics …
>
> And his head has also been full of readings from different instruments, of dotted lines on photographic paper that showed the trajectories of particles and the fission of nuclei.
>
> And there had even been room in his head for the rustling of leaves, the light of the moon, millet porridge with milk, the sound of flames in the stove, snatches of tunes, the barking of dogs, the Roman Senate, Soviet Information bulletins, a hatred of slavery, and a love of melon seeds.
>
> All this was what had given birth to his theory … And the logic of mathematics, itself quite unconnected with the world, had become reflected and embodied in a theory of physics; and this theory had fit with divine accuracy over a complex pattern of dotted lines on photographic paper.
>
> And Viktor, inside whose head all this had taken place, now sobbed and wiped tears of happiness from his eyes as he looked at the differential equations and photographic paper that confirmed the truth he had given birth to …
>
> How could he ever make sense of all this? … It's a strange feeling, you know. Whatever may happen to me now, I know deep down in my heart that I haven't lived in vain. Now, for the first time, I'm not afraid of dying … No, it's as though a lily had suddenly blossom out of still, dark waters … Oh, my God. (Ibid., 333–4)

Even if Grossman stresses the power of the mind, the initial richness and indetermination of experience (in which ideas are present as well as the melon seeds) emerges in the concrete adhering of ideas to the scribing of the photographic paper, until final truth rises from those sheets like a water lily in a dark pond.

Here there is no reference to the semiotic unity in a gesture because it is not represented, but the rest of the story shows that the theory created by Shtrum becomes a crucial technical experiment that has to be performed. The crucial experiment blends together the different kinds of signs. Crucial experiments are scientists' complete gestures. But the passage served to illustrate the phenomenological level that any practitioner of creativity, strictly understood, would recognize.

When creativity is at stake, there is no difference between the sciences and the arts. Creativity works in the same way, through the completeness of the phenomenological and the semiotic pattern that find their unity in gestures whose dense blending gives birth to that special creativity of artists and inventors.

## 4. PARTIAL CONCLUSIONS ON THE TOPIC

Finally, the pattern of complete gesture revealed in Grossman's literary work accounts for three experiences about creativity that common sense acknowledges. First, we understand that there is almost always something creative in ordinary gesture. In love, religion, work, education, science, and social commitment we are aware (and often happy) when there is some sort of creativity involved in what we are doing. At the same time, we understand that there is a difference between ordinary incomplete gestures, and complete gestures performed by those who we consider masters in their field. In chapter 5 I explained this difference from phenomenological and semiotic standpoints. Here I have shown what form complete gestures take when they are applied specifically to literature. The example shows us that in literary works – which are themselves gestures – there are incomplete and complete gestures that convey meaning with different power. This power difference is essential to understand, because incomplete gestures are as needed and valuable as complete ones. They communicate experience differently. The goal in this chapter was to stress that complete gestures are unique in offering a meaning (in a determinate form) so powerful that they can surpass the author's own thoughts and ability to convey them.

Second, the semiotic pattern that presides over gestures and complete gestures accounts for Tolkien's, Euler's, and many other great artists' and scientists' convictions about the fundamental role of the material act through which our thought develops. The saga of *The Lord of the Rings* stemmed from that first utterance because that statement was a complete gesture. Third, as far as it belongs to a complex development of experience through signs, creativity belongs much more to the whole reality in which we are immersed than to our singular geniuses. This explains why creativity on the one hand is perceived as a gift, and on the other hand is always an improvement on something that was in the air, something that builds on the thoughts of others and somehow belongs to the spirit of the time.

Certainly, this phenomenological and semiotic flux of reality is accepted, assented to, and fostered by singular individuals, by authors as subcreators, as we said in chapter 5. We established then that this authorship requires a normative aesthetic and ethical telos, and I am sure that further psychological studies are needed to ascertain when, where, and how the psyche enters the picture of synthetic reasoning through complete gestures. Nevertheless, the example of applied creativity has shown how much this authorship belongs to the phenomenological and semiotic flux of reality, and that it stems from experience.

# 8

# Gesture, Morality, Education

In the introduction I pointed out the threefold Kantian legacy that has blocked the road of philosophical inquiry in our epoch. The problem of necessity and the related distinction between analytic and synthetic judgment (and reasoning) have been tackled in the previous chapters. We have seen that a new definition of syntheticity arises following Peirce's mathematical and semiotic suggestions. This new definition relies upon the possibility of recognizing an identity through change. It stems from a different concept of continuity and change as the developing pattern of reality. This pattern is not reducible to the Kantian scheme of necessity. Analysis of this recognition brought to light the tool of complete gesture, as the phenomenological and semiotic synthetic structure for this synthetic reasoning. The work of this synthetic tool has been shown through examples; in the last three chapters I tried to enlarge the analysis of those complete gestures as it is applied to many important fields. In doing this, I noticed that the tool of complete gesture can be useful to understand our behaviours in many subtle fields of inquiry, such as personal identity, memory, and scientific and artistic creativity. Furthermore, these applications have clarified functions and dynamics of synthetic judgment and complete gesture.

In this clarification, the profound unity among disciplines appeared to be evident. Therefore, the third Kantian legacy listed in the introduction has already been dealt with and overcome in the last chapters. When one starts thinking according to a completely synthetic pattern, it so happens that discovery, invention, and artistic creativity merge. It is no longer possible to divide fields of experiences and disciplines in the way Kant, and the subsequent idealist and historicist philosophies, proposed.

A personal anecdote may illustrate this point. In 2008 I had the chance to participate in the conference "Discovery as Event" held in San Marino. Among the scholars there were C. Townes (a Nobel laureate for the discovery of the laser), J.C. Mather (Nobel laureate for the discovery of the cosmic microwave background radiation), J.C. Polkinghorne (Professor of Mathematical Physics at Cambridge, and theologian), O. Gingerich (Former Professor of History of Science at Harvard), and Y. Coppens (Collège de France, discoverer of the hominid Lucy). Contrary to the classic teaching on differences of methods and distinctions of sciences, they listed the following features as essential to research (in order of relevance to discovery): (1) sense of beauty; (2) dialogue; and (3) technology. They showed me that at high levels of inquiry, the analytic pattern with the distinction among disciplines is useless. Disciplines coalesce according to a mixture that we can now identify as the effort toward completion of gestures in a completely synthetic pattern of reasoning.

## 1. THE DISTINCTION BETWEEN THEORETICAL/PRACTICAL REASON. THE KANTIAN PATTERN AND THE PRAGMATIST REVOLT

Now it is time to tackle the second Kantian issue that I hinted at in the introduction: the Kantian legacy regarding the conception of morality. The Kantian pattern on this topic has been extremely influential throughout the history of the last two centuries, and greatly relevant to the division between disciplines that I mentioned above. In this section we will see that this distinction does not hold in a pragmatist account from the perspective of morality either. In the following sections I will also give some suggestions for a different view of the positive contents of morality in a philosophy of gesture.

As is well known, Kant's reconstruction of morality relies upon the fundamental distinction between the speculative and the practical use of pure reason. Pure reason belongs to the territory of experience, as defined by the word phenomenon. The denial of any possibility to consider the "thing in itself" is the strict border from which reason draws, in order to avoid metaphysical dreams and contradictions. According to the celebrated second edition of the *Critique of Pure Reason*, the "thing in itself" becomes an unknowable noumenon. Once this distinction is accepted, the paths of theoretical and practical uses are the opposite of one another. The theoretical use of pure reason has to follow the path that goes from sensibility as collected by intuition, to categories, principles, and apperception. The development of knowledge works from the exterior to the interior. The practical use of pure reason works the other way around: from the interior to the exterior. Its origin is the "fact" of the moral law that expresses the categorical imperative ("you must"), which is the core of our will. "Will" is the power to cause representations in the real world, even though this "causing" is only limited to the practical realm. Our will cannot change the rules settled by pure reason in its theoretical use: our knowledge of the phenomena teaches us that the phenomenal world is a completely deterministic world. However, our will witnesses and testifies that there is something that comes from another source, which is not the phenomenic world. Thus, "will" is the practical voice of inner noumenic freedom. Noumena are not knowable; therefore, we have to postulate noumenic freedom from the practical side of our pure reason. Freedom is the most effective power of the world, but only if knowledge is not mixed up with it. Kant despises every mixture of that kind, imposing the division among sciences and fields of inquiry that became normative for the Western world in the last two centuries.

A chasm, or in fact an abyss, opens up between the two realms of knowledge and freedom:

> In order to discover this condition of the application of the said concept [causality] to noumena, we need only recall why we are not content with its application to objects of experience, but desire also to apply it to things in themselves. It appears, then, that it is not a theoretic but a practical purpose that

> makes this necessity. In speculation, even if we were successful in it, we should not really gain anything in the knowledge of nature, or generally with regard to such objects as are given, but we should make a wide step from the sensibly conditioned ... to the supersensible, in order to complete our knowledge of principles and to fix its limits: whereas there always remains an infinite chasm unfilled between these limits and what we know: and we should have hearkened to a vain curiosity rather than a solid desire of knowledge. (Kant 1898, 144–5)

From the initial pattern that divides up, and assigns different roles to, practical and speculative reason, everything else follows. Practical reason affirms its freedom negatively by refusing any heteronomy and, positively, by adhering to the categorical imperative and to those laws that represent it (as showed by their necessity and universality). In this way morality has to be found only *in interiore hominis*, in the Kantian reformulation of Augustine's saw. However, the Kantian reformulation is as far as possible from Augustine: human beings cannot practice virtue for the sake of any reward, and duty – not desire – is the determinant reason for morality. Happiness is completely detached and extrinsic to morality, and can be postulated only insofar as the kingdom of God in a future life.

Pragmatist understanding of morality is far away from the Kantian picture. From the very naming of the movement (taken from Kant's anthropology), pragmatism wanted to bridge the gap between theory and practice, avoiding any dichotomy. Peirce did not pay much attention to morality, but other classic pragmatists did. James and Dewey were very active in this field, granting a pragmatist apparatus to this complex issue. James famously argued in favour of free will and put "choice" understood as selection as one of the most important values of his ethics (1912, 184–215).

Dewey dedicated a voluminous book to ethics. He argues for the necessity of critical thinking in order to ensure those satisfactory values that are so scarce in our lives. If those goods were everywhere, there would be no necessity of morality at all; but since goods are rare, we need critical thinking in order to decide what is moral, that is, what leads us to satisfaction (1932). James' and Dewey's understandings of morality reject the Kantian pattern. James did not maintain a substantive ethics. He suggested a pluralist exhortative form of ethics (Marchetti 2012a and 2012b), but the topic of selection related to attention is always present in his work. He connected it with attention and clearly inserted it into the epistemological pattern (James 1890). Knowledge itself cannot be but ethically committed. Notwithstanding the resistance found in the common Kantian perspective, Dewey went back to the definition of the link among happiness, morality, and understanding and to the importance of desire as a determinant reason for morality. Moreover, they both refused "an ethical philosophy made up in advance" (James 1896, 184). A-prioricity was not in the pragmatists' chords at all.

Recalling Peirce's understanding of ethics as a normative science that grounds logic,[1] it is difficult to imagine a position further away from Kant's. Knowledge and ethics are not only mixed up, but ethics is normatively necessary to logic, as aesthetics is to ethics. There is no reasoning without ethical and aesthetical judgments. Ethics and aesthetics judge reality from a cognitive point of view.[2] As we have seen, Peirce did not complete this view. He did not explain what concrete reasonableness is, except to describe it as "embodiment." However, it is clear that a pragmatist conception of ethics is far from Kantian divisions. Pragmatists understand that ethics can be normative, but this normativity is linked to a posteriori knowledge. And knowledge is always tied up with representation, and synthetically with action; or, in my view, with complete gestures.

## 2. VAGUENESS AND COMMON SENSE

Where the positive content of ethics is concerned, the pragmatist approach to ethics cannot be further from Kant's. Many themes could be interesting from this perspective: the recognition of happiness as the goal of ethical life, the sympathetic approach to desire and interest (even from the gnoseological point of view, as Peirce explains[3]), the acceptance of utility (even if in a broad sense, as a good verification of our ethical choices).

However, here I will concentrate my attention on the particular defense of common sense Peirce and James both made. I already hinted at it in chapter 1, but I want to be more precise here because this topic is extremely important in enabling us to understand one crucial difference from the Kantian pattern. I think that this difference establishes a watershed conception of morals.

The difference concerns common sense and common beliefs. Kant's ethics rely upon a deep denial of the usual view of ethics, which is based upon heteronomous determinant reasons and internal desire for happiness. The deep denial starts from the very idea of the *Critique of Pure Reason*: reason judges its own capacity and limits. When ethics is at stake, this critique implies the separation of the theoretical and the practical realms, and the refusal of sentiment and common sense as grounds for morality. The new formula that Kant proposes stems only from duty, and draws the concept of the good from the "I must" that is the core of the categorical imperative. In brief, this framework wants to criticize any tradition and any acceptance of it that would not be the universalizing rules of the *Critique* itself.

Classic pragmatists were strongly in favour of change to, and reconstruction of, morality. However, even in their most critical assessments, they did not despise heteronomy and they never stressed the role of the self.[4] On the contrary, they often doubted the importance of selfhood, and they questioned the substantial existence of the self. This attitude puts morality within a flux of reality in which selfhood is a function.[5] They defended the "reconstruction" of reality, but this approach also means that we are in a developmental reality in which we are not absolute masters. We can reform reality, but we cannot make it up. Paradoxically, for revolutionary thinkers, this theoretical perspective is also an unexpected defense of tradition, considered as the kind of reality that we receive or in which we are immersed. In this antithesis between tradition and not-tradition lies the core of a radical alternative to applied ethics.

What kind of tradition did pragmatists defend? Once again Peirce's picture is the most interesting, and it also accounts for the general pattern followed by the other classic pragmatists, who were possibly less aware of this common ground. Possibly the best of Peirce's account of common sense (and the morality based upon it) is showcased in the paper "Issues of Pragmatism" published in 1905. James read this paper, as evidenced by the letters between these two philosophers (L224, 15 October 1905), and he probably referred to it in his article "Pragmatism and Common Sense" published in the book *Pragmatism* (1907). In these letters the two founding fathers of pragmatism speak little about morality or about moral issues. But we already know that they intermingled knowledge and practice, so their comments on common sense are extremely significant for the moral field and are easily applied to it.

First of all, in these papers Peirce and James define common sense as the acceptance of some indubitable inferences (*EP2*, 347). Common sense does not limit itself to certain propositions, but it applies to fundamental ways of thinking. These fundamental ways are beyond critical control and "form one great stage of equilibrium in the human mind's development" (James 1907, 170). The corollary to this view of common sense is the famous anti-Cartesian standing on "paper doubts" and "living doubts" (*EP1*, 115). "Paper doubts" or Cartesian doubts are skeptical tricks to doubt in our heads what we do not doubt in our hearts, in order to rationalistically justify and exactly regain what we had (falsely) doubted. Living doubts witness our belonging to a flux of reality in which what we receive is a certainty, which is the base for any further step. Insofar as we are surrounded by these certainties, we can fairly doubt something when experience itself shows some unexpected phenomenon. In this case we question our previous explanations, only to acquire a new certainty.

Peirce and James agree on a second characteristic of the defense of common sense: its evolving constitution. Common sense is our first acknowledgment of experience and, since experience evolves, it evolves too. The evolution of common sense is slow. If these certainties evolve, they are not a priori: James thought they were "discovered" by some genius in the past; Peirce attributed them to "rational instinct," considered to be the first stage of hypothetical inquiry, so that certainty was once again a "discovery." The a-priorism that Kant considered to be the indubitable feature of reason is here questioned and denied.

James stops at that point and follows another thread. He connects common sense to science, and casts some shadow on the former as a reflex of his suspicion on the latter. However, the acceptance of common sense as reasoning and part of reality is already accomplished. Peirce goes into the depth of his conception. His (critical) common sensism implies a logical analysis. The certainties of common sense are vague, in a strict logical sense of the term. As we have learned in previous chapters, according to Peirce, vague means that the sign is objectively undetermined. We would need a further determination by the utterer. Peirce contrasts vagueness with generality, where the sign needs a further determination by the interpretant. In a more scientific way, "anything is general in so far as the principle of excluded middle does not apply to it and is vague in so far as the principle of contradiction does not apply to it" (*EP2*, 351). Evolution means that there are also transitions between logical modalities, so that something that is vague can become general.

This logical/ontological transition is quite important for understanding pragmatism's profound departure from Kant's morality. Our inherited morality – that is, our tradition – is vague but this does not mean that it is not true or not justified. The belief in God for example is as vague as possible. Its vagueness is rather a proof of its importance and reality than an objection to it. Common sense has to be criticized, but its first vague suggestion is the richest background of any development of thought. Peirce accepted that this scheme also belongs to morality, and he used to say that he was for a "sentimental conservatism" in ethics (*CP* 1.661). James advocated the same view when he held that we should be epistemically conservative[6] and that we can even postulate a divine thinker in order to live our strenuous moral life (1896, 213–14). A few positive items are the core of this conservatism.

However, what is important to our goal in this chapter is the inversion of Kant's pattern in a double sense: 1) unity of speculation and practice and 2) acceptance of our unavoidable belonging to the development of reality. It is easy to understand that this acceptance involves both tradition and reconstruction. Only in this way can Peirce's sentimental conservatism and Dewey's reconstructive ethics be understood adequately. In fact, it is when one understands that we belong to a broader stream of experience that James's paradoxical, contemporaneous statements about the importance both of "conservatism" and of "breaking rules" become intelligible. Immersed in the flux of experience, we are both receivers as well as developers of currents made of ideals, thoughts, emotions, states of things, and satisfactions. A pragmatist account explains both the pluralistic openness to different choices and the final destination of this huge stream of experience. For pragmatists there is no absolute ethics, but skepticism is completely forbidden. They know that experience, judged a posteriori, can indicate the direction to truth, even though we cannot know it all by now. An ideal last day, when the last man "has had his experience and said his say," would coincide with the sum of all conceivable experience, and thus it would show what truth is (James 1896, 184). In this opposition – between realism as the awareness of belonging to evolutionary reality, and nominalism as a static moral a-priorism – lies the most significant contribution of pragmatism to the conception of morality. Now I will use the tool of complete gesture to supplement Peirce's and classic pragmatists' view. The pattern of morality based on complete gestures will build upon the profound unity between knowledge and practice that classic pragmatists proposed, putting it into our completely synthetic turn.

## 3. ETHICAL EPISTEMOLOGY. A DEFINITION OF MORALITY BASED ON COMPLETE GESTURES

Why should the tool of complete gesture represent an advance in the conception of morality? Complete gesture shows a very important change in the conception of morality because it perceives morality within the pattern of creation of the action itself. Morality becomes an intrinsic value of knowledge instead of an external discipline.

How does this involvement happen? As in the case of the epistemic view of complete gesture, I am going to give a definition. It will be as rich and descriptive as possible, but it is always and only a definition with some examples. The paradox is that a gesture is a kind of reasoning that should be and is performed, but words are the only way to talk about it. However, I hope that this definition, and the illustrative examples that accompany it, will help clarify the structure of morality of what happens as complete gesture.

We know that the complete gesture, understood as a phenomenological and semiotic plexus, is an epistemic tool that unites practice and theory, knowledge and communication. When we perform a gesture, we do not apply some previous concept, but we comprehend something more or new in the action of gesture itself. We have seen that in the complete gesture, the complexity of ideas becomes actual and possibly necessary, but this "becoming" cannot happen without complete gestures. As is true in the whole pragmatist tradition, Kant's distinction between practical and speculative realms does not apply here. Practice is the way in which we know synthetically, a posteriori and not a priori. Complete gestures show that knowing is a form of recognizing or, in words taken from the normative conditions expressed in chapter 5, a form to answer the question that reality asks: "Don't you think so?"[7] Our performance of an action densely composed of firstness, secondness, and thirdnesss, and of icons, indices, and symbols is the how that answer happens.

In effect, complete gestures are the form of our participation in the concrete development of experience. The tool of complete gesture is born into the idea of continuity. This original birth is testified to by the pattern of creativity that I described in chapter 5: we belong to a tradition understood as the flux of reality. Complete gestures receive the experience of reality in a certain form and help in modifying it. Again, the way in which they receive reality is often vague, and according to the modality of possibility, they actually modify it within existence. They transform it into a habit of action, giving rise to new interpretations. Therefore, tradition and reconstruction are the two poles of the same developing whole.

### 3.1 *Selection and Teleology*

When we perform a complete gesture, with all the specifications we saw in the previous chapters, we do judge that one possibility out of many is worth being actualized, to the point that we make it an aim expressed in a habit of action. We cited a few examples: the purification bath, the artistic performance in Grossman, mountaineers' stone carrying, Rutherford's gold foil experiment. In all these cases, according to different shapes, *an* experience has to be read according to a possibility that becomes actual and then a habit of action. In all examples, gestures grasp an idea that they want to represent and foster: the idea of purification, the equality between totalitarianisms, the importance of learning how to behave on the mountains, the structure of atoms. Among an infinite number of possibilities, complete gestures select (in a very Jamesean attitude) one actualization. Why do they select that particular form of representation? Why does purification have to become a bath, totalitarian uniformity take the form of the dialogue between Liss and Mostovskoy, the educational behaviour take the form of carrying a stone, and a hypothesized structure of atoms take the form of an experiment? The form of representation is selected according to the criterion of better fitting the general order of signs.

As pointed out by James and Mead, ethics is called for in this part of the action, while the acquaintance with the general order of signs can be analytically listed under the discipline of aesthetics. This order must coincide with our final goal. In gestures the aim is included within the gesture itself, thanks to the symbolic thirdness that it must include. In this way aesthetics, ethics, and logic form one and the same tool, which is useful to comprehend, to judge, to communicate, and to admire.

Technically speaking the ethical judgment of plausibility applies to possibilities, actualities, and habits of actions. In addition it applies to icons, indices, and symbols, accepting those signs that are more fitted to represent both the initial vagueness and the final general aim of the experience that we want to know, change, and foster. Any complete gesture comports a meaning that is the outcome of choices. Those choices represent a general ideal, bringing it from initial vagueness to a specific determination and a replicable meaning. Insofar as it carries a meaning, any complete gesture will shed light upon the ideal that the gesture itself wants to realize.

We understand the power of this model when we realize that the complete gesture as a whole, by virtue of the internal ethical judgment, displays the conception that we want to represent. Morality becomes "the relationship between the gesture and the conception of the totality implied in the gesture" (Giussani 1998, 80). This reflexivity that comes from ontological continuity is essential to the paradigm, and casts light upon its richness and power. The point is that any action can be more or less moral according to the degree in which it becomes a complete gesture. A complete gesture is a moral gesture in its complete realization of the vague idea and general ideal it wants to express. This approach also means that any activity can be moral if it realizes its own ideal. Any action, bad action included, can be moral insofar as it embodies its vague initial idea and its general final ideal.

Here a question arises about summum bonum – the highest ideal to which any ideal can aspire, and a subject that falls beyond the scope of this book. However, from the perspective of complete gestures, we can derive a little hint of the direction that studies on summum bonum will have to take. The broader the horizon of the signs embraced by the vague idea and the general ideal, the more the gesture can synthetize in its singularity. The broader the horizon, the denser will be the complete gesture that embodies it. This is probably the best sense we can make of Peirce's idea of concrete reasonableness as ideal, and of the general order of signs that serves as a criterion of choice. The more any aesthetical understanding takes into account a plurality of complete gestures (tradition and evolution) the more it will fit the order, meaning the more effective it will be. Reasonableness is the most comprehensive horizon of knowledge of which the human mind can think and that complete gestures prefigure.

### 3.2 *Neither Dogmatism nor Relativism*

In this model, ethical rationalism is avoided as much as is ethical empiricism; or, in more contemporary terms, ethical dogmatism is avoided as much as is ethical relativism. How so? Complete gestures do not imply any "dogma"[8] because they are not an application of an a priori pattern or set of rules: they are an embodiment of a vague background and tradition. Moreover, any performance of a complete gesture is different from any other in virtue of its secondness and indexicality, so that any mere application is impossible.

Since any performance is a new comprehension, it is impossible to pre-determine what exactly the outcome will be. The problem with actions that are mere copies – even in artistic performances – is that there is no more novelty: in performing them we do not comprehend anything new, and hence they do not hold our interest. The case of regime newspapers is a good example of this lack of novelty. Another example is our disillusionment when we find out that a piece of artwork is a copy; we realize it lacks new comprehension within it. A third example is the sense of uneasiness one might have during "formalities," an uneasiness that stems from the lack of novelty in their re-performance. When they are original re-performances, they are not formal habits anymore.[9] There is no dogma (in the trivial sense of the word) in performing complete gestures.

On the other hand, the outcome is not open to just any solution. Initial vagueness, ethically judged and physically performed, obliges the outcome into some interpretative paths: not simply any path is allowed. You can take the dialogue between Liss and Mostovskoy as a dialogue that exemplifies the ideology-freedom issue instead of the State-individual issue. But you cannot say that the dialogue shows that Nazis were worse than communists. There are certain boundaries of interpretative freedom permitted by the singularity of any performance and by the symbolicity that any gesture implies.[10] This does not mean that symbols are detached or severed from the initial experience, or separated from the meaning that the gesture in its totality carries out. Meaning is increased and modified by complete gestures, but there is a general direction that is determined by the initial vague comprehension of experience and by the general aim we want to attain. This teleology, put into place by the author of the gesture, accompanies all the realizations and cannot be totally subverted.[11] Mere empiricism and mere relativism are excluded by the presence of the aim that thirdness and symbolicity bring to any complete gesture.

Complete gestures are tools for our synthetic understanding of morality as a developing experience that moves between tradition and reconstruction. They positively assume, and critically change, the values of tradition. They represent a goal that they themselves help to provide as a modification of tradition. Let us take, for example, gay marriage. The issue does not only consist of rights desired by a certain part of society; otherwise, those rights would easily be granted. The two parties that debate this issue are correctly focusing on that one gesture, which, if performed or not performed, would concretize and synthetize their own ideals. So, this debate is part of the transition between tradition and reconstruction. Nobody is questioning the vague traditional ideals and values of loyalty, companionship, and togetherness. The point is whether to – and how to – reconstruct these traditional ideals according to the goal of universalization or to the goal of diversification of functions and kinds of love. The moral discussion is thus comprehensible, and the outcome will shape our understanding (through a complete gesture) of what kind of society we will be tomorrow.

The tool of complete gesture accounts for the importance that each party involved in the discussion ascribes to that one gesture, and illuminates (and compels us to change) previous vague ideals into more general terms. Being a logical tool, complete gesture does not say what is morally right or wrong, but it tells us what we have in common and what is at stake. Finally, complete gestures tell us that morality is not a priori and cannot be merely formal.[12]

## 4. RATIONAL AND MORAL INSTINCT

Even without addressing the problem of the ultimate goal's content (whether it is ultimate and which will be its positive determination), we already know that any particular complete gesture implies an ideal or aim that is ultimate according to a particular field or experience.[13]

The relationship among "aims" is the aesthetic issue that I decided not to touch upon in this book, although the breadth of the system of signs that reasoning considers is a good starting point for future research. However, it is impossible not to hint at another problem: who is judging? Who is moral? Who is the subject of the ethical judgment at any level?

In chapter 5 I noted that there must be an author in order to have a complete gesture. In this chapter, I wish to add to the notion of complete gesture by showing the ethical-logical subjectivity of this author. Let us use Peirce's insights one more time. Very acutely Peirce informs us that "will" or voluntariness cannot be the source of self-control (*EP2*, 200). In other passages he identifies this source of judgment as the attunement between our rationality and the development of reality. He calls it a "rational instinct." My previous studies have shown that Peirce pondered this topic until the very late years of his life, connecting it more and more with the ground of rationality. He started with a description of it as "hope" (1901), and then he identified it as reasonable "insight" (1903), "rational instinct" (1908), and "intellectual instinct" (1911).[14] According to my reconstruction of Peirce's theory of abduction, the function of this rational instinct is to say "yes" to the proposal of reality ("don't you think so?") when we have to decide whether to accept a hypothesis as an explanation for some surprising phenomenon that broke our previous certainties.

The biblical tradition names this ultimate ground of any judgment as "heart" (*lebab*) without opposing sentiment and rationality. "Heart" is exactly what seems to come from the Peircean tradition: a ground for judgment in both speculative and practical matters. True enough, this consideration does not hold for all pragmatists, and on this topic they diverge much more than on any other. James, Dewey, and Mead seem to hold an even less substantial view of the source of judgment, identifying it with the change of reality itself, or with a specific adaptation of reality slightly modified by attention or choice (Dewey 1925, Mead 1934, James 1904).[15]

Regardless, the tool of complete gesture requires a more substantial vision of the faculty of judgment, and I will take the idea of rational instinct or "heart" as this aesthetical-ethical-logical function. We have already identified the object of this faculty: the plausibility of some possibility (in abduction) or of some embodiment of possibility according to a general ideal (complete gesture). As for the method, we said that logically and semiotically speaking it is an acceptance or refusal of a certain plausible representation. This dual possibility of an answer displays the very specific characteristics of rational instinct: it can accept or refuse, but it cannot imagine the content of the answer. It works on a semiotic path that presents itself to its celebrated "gates," but it cannot make up the content of representation itself. It can say "good" and "bad," exactly as at the other gate it can only say "true" or "false." Socrates recognized something similar when he was talking about the demon that forbade him to do certain actions (Ap. Soc. 31d). Rational instinct and "heart" have a more important function than Socrates' demon: they work not only as negative alarms but also as acceptations or positive recognizing.

Does this function hint at an ontological self? For now it is possible to answer, with all pragmatists, that I am describing a "function." I think that this question goes beyond the limit of the complete gesture tool and the model of reasoning based on it. In this book I am more committed to describing the synthetic embodiment of ideals than to analyzing possible metaphysical origins or ends.

## 5. EDUCATION

Following the description that I gave, any gesture has its own inner morality, which is necessary to achieve its synthetic knowledge. However, the ethical and educational methods implied in complete gestures are the same, independent of the ideal embodied in them.

### *5.1 Re-performance*

The first methodological characteristic is that the view of morality combined with knowledge, as I described, implies re-performance. I use this term to avoid "repetition," which is different and belongs to the category of incomplete gestures for lack of iconicity.[16] If morality is lived and known through complete gestures, the way to apprehend it is by re-performing. Odd as it can sound to our rationalist ears, morality is learned more as we learn to ski or to swim than as we read a textbook.

Re-performance is at the heart of possible novelty as well. Like jazz musicians (Colapietro 2013), only those who are immersed into a tradition – who have learned complete gestures – can improvise in a fruitful manner and change the tradition with a series of different or alternative complete gestures.

## 5.2 *Master and Critique*

The conception of morality that stems from this philosophy of gestures involves the presence of a master. Certainly, this characteristic opens up all problems connected to power and manipulation. I set aside these problems that need further studies, and instead I will concentrate on the necessity of a master. The master, who wants to convey or transfer ideas about morality, is the one who decides what complete gestures to perform so that others can understand. Besides, he has to perform the complete gestures in front of the student and with the student. Since actors are different, performances are different from one another, and there is no mere repetition of the same gesture. This same co-participation with complete gesture obliges the master to change at each performance and with every student. This description accounts for the sense of novelty and satisfaction that teachers and masters of any field feel. When this sentiment disappears, teaching has lost some element and is not complete anymore.

Finally, the master has to critically judge his own and the student's performances. As we have seen, critique is implied by the idea of completion. To be complete a gesture must present a dense blending of phenomenological and semiotic elements, and this density has to be ethically judged according to how these elements fit the general order of signs. Any performance of a complete gesture (taking for granted that they are never the same) can be a further or nearer approximation of the aim we want to embody. On the other hand, the student or the pupil (at any age in any field) will learn by performing with the master. This form of learning is by identifying oneself with another or by putting oneself in another's shoes.[17]

## 5.3 *Fallibilism and Time*

The third important characteristic of morality based on gestures is approximation. "Completion" of gesture does not mean that there is a final version of a complete gesture; since they are always a historical realization, they depend on the situation (space, time, actors) and cannot be definitive. Lacking a final version, gestures can only be judged by comparing them; therefore, judgments have to be open to ever new and more perfect realizations.

"Openness" or "questioning" is thus the moral face of fallibilism (remember the line of ter-identity and its loose end). To question whether there is another possibility of embodiment, to strive for completion and afterward discern whether another situation would ask for a new complete form, and to ask experts for guidance are all distinctive features of this synthetic conception of morality. These have to be taken into account in any form of education.

The philosophical problem of time is implied in the theme of fallibilism. Infinite openness implies infinite time for realization. This does not mean that there is no direction or improvement. As discussed before, complete gestures have a direction in themselves, since they are teleologically oriented. Therefore, they strive for a final embodiment, which is ultimately impossible because of the vague ground of possibilities on which firstness and iconicity rely. We have fair and fairer realizations. We can have successful performances, and those successes will be imitated and sometimes critically ameliorated. But we cannot have a final perfect performance that would coincide with complete embodiment or complete truth.

In other words, if time and social relationships are implied we could say that morality is a story: a story made of complete gestures. The kind of continuity that this story displays is the one we learned in previous chapters: a non-metric continuity based on the structural properties of complete gestures that synthetize ideas and events as time goes by.

## CONCLUSION: PRAGMATIST IMITATION

This notion of moral education through the use of complete gestures takes advantage of the imitative power of human beings.[18] The uniqueness of this power has often been questioned in the last century.[19] However, significant accounts based on scientific experiments have proven that in human beings, imitation is different from the apparently similar imitation by other animals (apes, above all). Tomasello (1999) has distinguished them by the names of "imitation" and "emulation." Apes emulate gestures, namely, they choose to repeat an action by looking at its result, without determining the intention of the person whom they are emulating. Conversely, in the first months of life, human beings learn to look for the intention of a gesture, even though the gesture does not lead to the result immediately. They keep imitating even when the gesture is not the fastest way to the goal. In a very Husserlian phenomenological view, Tomasello reads this capacity as the product of human intentionality that permits humans to look at others and consider them to be "like me."[20] Thus, German phenomenology bridges the gap between one's isolated mind and other minds in order to avoid solipsism.

The hypothesis that this pragmatist approach would formulate in order to interpret the same characteristic of human beings traverses in the opposite direction, since pragmatism thinks of human beings as completely immersed in the flux of reality. From this perspective human beings are also imitating and not emulating. This imitation, however, is not because they ascribe to others a shared intent according to an analogy, but because they identify themselves with others by interpreting their gestures, thinking that "I belong to them" or "I am like them." When I see others perform a gesture, I repeat in myself the same path; re-performing the same gesture means to learn it by doing, but also to learn to recognize the same identity through change that others recognize. In other words, we are in the same flux of reality and we learn what we are from others by actions that mean something. We are attracted by the power to shape reality that others demonstrate, and we want to participate with the same power. This is the way in which the theoretical "admirableness" reaches into our daily lives: we want to be like someone else, and we discover that we have to ask and learn. The validity of this idea is testified by the fact that human babies first discover reality outside themselves, and only secondarily do they learn to recognize themselves. This self-recognition is almost through recognition of difference from the totality, and perhaps also because they experience their own private impotence within that surrounding reality.

The perspective of knowledge is now turned upside-down. We are not the independent masters of detached reality. Indeed it is other way around: we are part of a reality with which we cooperate inasmuch as we imitate its intention by learning to perform the complete gestures taught by others. Grossman grasped this paradoxical nature of the universe when he described the first spatial flight beyond the atmosphere by a living being, a little dog by the name of Petrushka: "what was special was the presence of a living being, penetrating the cosmos with her psyche. Or rather the other way around – the cosmos would penetrate the psyche of a living being .... The psyche of a living creature would be penetrated by another kingdom – a kingdom not covered by the warmth of the earth, by soft cumulus clouds, by the damp power of phlogiston" (2010, 266). This cosmological realist premise leads us to understand the fallible, limited role of our individual selves, as Shakespeare said (and Peirce re-performed):

> But man, proud man,
> Dressed in a little brief authority,
> Most ignorant of what he's most assured,
> His glassy essence, like an angry ape
> Plays such fantastic tricks before high heaven
> As makes the angels weep.[21]

# Conclusions and Further Studies

## 1. THE NOVELTY OF THE PATTERN

In the case of this book, conclusions are really an invitation for future investigation. When you usher in a new paradigm of research you can explore its implications over the course of many decades, following very different threads of thought, or you can publish the rough draft of the new idea when it reaches a sufficient determination, hoping that there will be many scholars from different fields who are interested in verifying its results and relevance. There have been many examples of both approaches in the history of philosophy. I have pursued the latter option.

This chapter will be a list of topics and suggestions rather than a real conclusion. I hope that this text will serve as an introductory work. However, before listing new fields and topics, I want to underscore again the usual way of conceiving reasoning that this paradigm has subverted.

The goal here was to give a more faithful account of what reason and reasoning are. Previous studies with an analytic understanding of Peirce and pragmatism convinced me that there was something missing in their picture of reasoning. Pragmatists were really innovative thinkers. What puzzled me was that they kept finding points of experience in which we need some reasoning different from the usual pattern established by past schools of philosophy: the connection with practice, the abductive process, the system of signs, the relevance of interpretation without arbitrariness, and the externalism of meaning. Notwithstanding their brilliant achievements, they could not figure out a satisfactory picture of reasoning into which all of their findings could fit. I used to call these curious borders of reasoning "vanishing points," referring to where pragmatists seemed to lean on a completely different territory, like when you go to the top of a high mountain: at the very end you discover, on the other side of the rock or the glacier, new valleys, rivers, mountains, and maybe the sea far away. Such was my journey in the philological study of pragmatism. At the end of any analytic pattern, classic pragmatists also foresaw the valley of a completely different pattern of reasoning – without really believing in it. I named this pattern "synthetic," as a tribute to the philosophical tradition, but what I meant was something different from the traditional notion of "synthetic."

The new pattern required a redefinition of the analytic pattern, and indeed there was no other solution: when you discover a new land, new definitions arise, and previously known lands must also be redefined in relation to the new one. Besides new and old lands, a fair consideration of the unique nature of the border itself, where the passage on the ridge suggested an important change, is needed. In homage to Peirce and following many other authors I called this zone (which will need much more attention than what I could give it during the journey of this book) "vague." The discipline of "horotics" (the study of *horos*, borders) has yet to come to light.

As explained in chapter 3, the new paradigm conceives synthesis as "recognition of an identity through changes," redefining analysis as "losing an identity through changes" and accepting vagueness as the situation of "blindness to identity through changes." The complicated story told in chapter 3 about the nature of change and recognition ends in proposing that the synthetic result A=B is the original form of recognizing of identity, of which the analytic A=A is only a degenerate case. In the middle, between the two, and somehow before them, there is the vague zone of passage, the nature and borders of which will be the first topic of my "to-do" list.

In many ways there are antecedents of my position. Heraclitus, Augustine, Blaise Pascal, Hegel, F.W.J. Schelling, Owen Barfield, and Martin Heidegger are only the most famous of those who saw that there should be this "other" territory. They hinted at its existence and indicated that it was related to the – already known – analytic land in a special way; but they could not describe any rational pattern for it, nor did they question and focus the rationale of the passing area of vagueness.

As I mentioned, the idea of looking at this new land came from philological studies on Peirce and pragmatism, as well as my encounter with the Colombian mathematician Fernando Zalamea. His work helped me see that from a mathematical standpoint, the analytic pattern had been overtaken many years ago, and that philosophy is still thinking according to a mathematical paradigm that has been deemed correct but limited. In philosophy, the analytic paradigm is also simply exhausted. Having furnished valid tools and good results in many fields, it is now stuck in an arid scholasticism. It is time to put this old pattern into a broader picture, exactly as happened to Newton's theory when the theory of relativity was discovered, or to post-Gödel mathematics. The opening of new fields saved the validity of the traditional teaching, even if this validity was limited to certain fields and perspectives.

Once I understood the new synthetic pattern as "recognition of an identity" and followed the insights of Peirce's existential graphs, I identified the rational tools necessary for a new paradigm of philosophy known as complete gesture. This new philosophical approach creates a new space for research. Complete gesture is a tool that makes us see universals into particular actions defined by Peirce's kind of continuity – as described by (Zalamea 2001) – and a special (dense) blending of phenomenological and semiotic characteristics. Once again, it was a great joy to discover that the tool of "gesture" had already been mentioned by the same philosophers of mathematics. These were the same ones who understood the limitation of the analytic pattern. As Peirce said, absolute novelty would be almost certainly an error – and definitely not communicable.

By comprehending complete gestures we also understand the incompleteness of gestures. We may account for many different levels and nuances of phenomenological and semiotic structures of the new land. After this first perusal, the new soil seems to be more akin to the one in which our common sense moves, rather than to the complicated structures of the analytic pattern. We could say that the new completely synthetic pattern is the rational root of our common sense and common living. This is why the philosophy of complete gesture finds so many applications and, by nature of this embodied philosophy itself, any application illustrates the pattern and the tool better. Memory, personal identity, artistic creativity, morality, and education have been presented in this book as examples of applications, because they seemed more immediately relevant for our understanding. But there are many other fields and topics that should be worked through the philosophy of gesture. The first ones that come to my mind include philosophy of mathematics (of course), communication, sociology, psychology (is there a psycho-synthesis? I think so), law, anthropology, and politics.[1] I am sure it will apply to many others, and it is important to notice that in any field, we have a tool available to view comprehension as given through, or givable through, action. Comprehension really can be conceived of as a non-rationalist affair, just as classic pragmatists dreamed.

This task is going to occupy a long period of time. I am fully aware of the introductory character of this book and, even more, of the mere suggestiveness of these concluding remarks. However, I want to list topics that are immediately relevant to the pattern but which I could not yet pursue.

## 2. HOROTICS: THE LOGIC OF VAGUENESS

One of the most fascinating characteristics of the new paradigm is its triadic form (instead of the usual binary one). The completely synthetic pattern requires room for vagueness as a third realm or territory alongside analysis and synthesis. This finding stems from the new definition/description of the two territories. As reported in chapter 4, we can move from analysis to synthesis and vice versa. Usually, the moment of passage is really different from both forms of reasoning and, having its own laws, must be a reasoning in itself. The vagueness that we detected is a point in which we are completely blind to the identity of the changing reality. Analytically, it is the moment that we enter those "vanishing points" in which the object of inquiry has been dissolved. Synthetically, it is the area of reasoning from which we receive meanings to embody in complete gestures. Existentially, it is the moment of contradiction, of open possibilities, of undetermined, rough, and strong beliefs. For example, in the last chapter I mentioned that common sense is always vague, and in this vagueness lays its richness. Vagueness is logically and ontologically the world of possibilities, namely a world in which the principle of contradiction does not hold. There is no swinging between analysis and synthesis that does not require vagueness. I am inclined to think that any knowledge begins, philogenetically, as vague. The territory of vagueness or horotics is thus as uberous or fecund as it is confused.

The problem with horotics is the same one we had with synthetic reasoning: we need a proper tool to research it, because if we use the analytic tools of philosophical tradition we cannot grasp it. As a matter of fact the tool of inquiry modifies results, so that we need an appropriate tool for every field. The turning point of our studies on synthesis took place when we found a synthetic tool for it, rather than the analytic tools that had always been used. As I said in the introduction, this was also the weakness of the pragmatists: they strove for synthesis but they could not escape the analytic pattern and its tools. Now for horotics we need a vague tool: a vague tool to inquire about vagueness. So far I have not found a good tool for this research, although I have found many possible points of departure: studies on iconicity and contradiction, mathematical intuitionism, topological breaking points, Schelling's ecstasy, and Florensky's awe. The logic of vagueness will then eventually segue into the ontological study of it, even though that time seems out of reach right now.

## 3. A POSTERIORI METAPHYSICS

Talking about ontology and metaphysics, the completely synthetic pattern discovered in this book suggests the hypothesis of a posteriori foundationalism, a strange creature in a pragmatist environment.

Pragmatism has often been connected with anti-foundationalism and anti-metaphysics. However, if foundationalism is understood properly as the "thesis that criteria of justification are not purely conventional but stand in need of objective grounding, being satisfactory only if truth-indicative (i.e. which takes criteria of justification to be founded by their relation to truth)" (Haack 2009, 244), doubts arise about when one adopts this synthetic pattern. On my account, pragmatism is consistent with the possibility of foundationalism about justification – or foundherentism as advocated by Haack – but there is also room for a real Foundationalism (capitalized for respecting Haack's distinctions). Sure enough, pragmatists were not for a priori Foundationalism, which they found a useless intellectualist model into which rationalist thinkers try to shrink reality. However, their insistence on continuity and on the connection between conceivable effects and truth hints toward a paradoxical but very interesting a posteriori foundation of knowledge. I know that this view is hard to conceive, but it is not quite impossible if you make use of the mathematical model. As both contemporary philosophy of mathematics and Wittgenstein claimed, the foundation of mathematics comes through our doing mathematics. Peirce was well aware of this paradox, and that is why he was not scared by the results of Cantor's and Russell's antinomies. Since we do mathematics, there is a foundation. If it works, it is. You cannot find an a priori logical and ontological foundation, but this does not mean we cannot find them at all. Once you have drawn your graphs, the Foundation is somehow attained in the graph itself. So the question of further studies will be: is a posteriori Foundationalism possible? If it were so, how would that Foundationalism would be justified?

This consideration was also at the beginning of my speculation on gestures and their characteristics. We have seen that in any gesture, and in complete gestures in particular, a number of vague meanings are embodied in an action so that they become evident and general at the same time. Complete gestures are synthetic because they embody universals in particular actions. In effect, we can understand the meaning of an expression or recognize a certain identity by performing gestures. Does this phenomenological and semiotic structure entail an ontological, a posteriori Foundation? An a priori Foundation is still impossible because gestures follow the continuous change of reality, and they cannot be predicted or syllogistically deduced. But are they part of this change as well? Do they participate in ontological change?

Those are good questions for future research. For now, I say that I would not find it strange if that were the case. Are we not always inventing or building or creating new objects, whether they be possible as dreams, actual as cell phones, necessary as characters in a play? Do we build ontologies as they are built in the constructivist pattern? Our synthetic land seems to incline us toward cooperation, a limited but real capacity of reforming ontologies. We are "sub-creators," Tolkien used to say. Certainly, it is an odd position and only several studies in diverse fields (mathematics, physics, biology, genetics, and theology are the first to come to my mind) could justify it.

A corollary of this inquiry should be the study of evolution. If complete gestures modify the ontological structure of reality, a different picture of evolutionism has to emerge. Peirce contrasted the differences between Lamarckism and Darwinism metaphorically by noting that the former was an evolutionism by love while the latter an evolutionism by greed. Outside the metaphor, Peirce's idea was that habits actively modify biology and evolution. The idea was falsified by further scientific research. However, in the last few years, bio-semiotics re-introduced various teleological components into the understanding of biological processes. Is there a different way to look at evolution from a completely synthetic point of view? Connected to this question, can the anthropological threshold be more understandable from the standpoint of complete gestures?

## 4. PSYCHOLOGY AND ETHICS

In our dealing with complete gestures, we maintained the necessity of assent that we tackled from a semiotic standpoint and, partially, from an ethical perspective. In chapter 5 we stated that there must be a psychological component in assenting to the dense or loose blending of phenomena and signs. Whether the intervention of psychology is limited to the point of assent, or to an entire third structure of completion of gesture, a structure that could be built upon the classic triad of feeling, attention, or cognition (or some contemporary reformulation of it) is a matter that I am not expertly prepared to answer. A keen knowledge of psychological studies is needed in order to give a plausible answer. For now and for me it is enough to ask the question.

Certainly, the possible positive application of the philosophy of gesture on a therapeutic level is a hint toward the recognition of an entirely different psychological structure than the phenomenological and the semiotic ones. The paradigm of complete gestures can help our understanding of foundationally significant moments in the development of personalities. For better and for worse, we build our personalities through complete gestures (ch. 6) and this comprehension can help healing or recovering with positive gestural therapies. If it were so, it would be plausible to hypothesize that there are psychological structures at work in complete gestures.

As far as ethics is concerned, I ascertained and maintained the existence of ethical intervention within the semiotic (logic) formation of complete gestures (ch. 6). In chapter 8 I also cast a glance toward a positive version of ethics. Nonetheless in both cases a question on the nature of, and the method to reach, summum bonum appeared. As for the first aspect – the "pure" one, Peirce used to say – the philosophy of gesture requires the ethical assent that judges aesthetical admirableness, but at the end we could not really understand with what this admirableness coincided. Peirce's translation of admirableness into "concrete reasonableness" is a clue about the synthetic direction that the founder of pragmatism was taking, but the problem remains.

When ethics was taken in a positive sense, we saw that completion of gestures implies an inner morality: one is moral as much as he/she performs a complete gesture, namely he/she embodies into a gesture a vague meaning until it becomes determined and able to display that meaning according to universality and evidence. In this way one can be moral in performing anything – from burglary and homicide to self-sacrifice, one can be moral in his/her performance. But of course the meaning that we embody in one complete gesture is part of a complex net of complete gestures that form reality. That a gesture is fostering reality and knowledge in one sense or in another is not the same from both a pure and applied ethical perspective. I think that in this question, which amounts to the celebrated and ancient issue of summum bonum, the gap closes between the gnoseological view of ethics and its practical consequences. What we have in both cases is again a teleological view, and it has to be elaborated carefully and in conjunction with the metaphysical study itself. What is this summum bonum to which aesthetics and ethics refer and aim? Is it some sort of phenomenological/semiotic totality, like the gesture of all gestures? If it is so, it must be very different from the analytic totality that antinomies showed to be a fallacious entity.

These three topics could help finish the picture of complete gesture that I started in this book. The discovery of this completely synthetic pattern and its main tool has been of great help to answer the question about the unity of theory and practice that has always accompanied my approach to knowledge. I hope that this proposal will be considered and tested by the community of inquirers, and I am sure that this consideration will improve what I have said so far. I know that improvements can also be critical, and that my own criticism can even reveal angles that I never saw, angles that can eventually make us reject the hypothesis. However, everything I have written is the result of many years of study and dialogue of philosophy as complete gesture.

# Notes

## INTRODUCTION

1 See Levinas 1961, 19–20.
2 Willard Van Orman Quine (1908–2000) criticized the synthetic/analytic distinction in his seminal paper "Two Dogmas of Empiricism" (1951). His work often hinted at pragmatism as a possible way out of the paradoxes of a strict analytic tradition.
3 Protagoras of Abdera (ca. 490–ca. 420 BCE) is well known for his doctrine according to which "Of all things the measure is Man, of the things that are, that they are, and of the things that are not, that they are not" (DK 80B1). A utilitarian reading of it has often been proposed during the history of philosophy.
4 Cf. De Tienne 2009.
5 See also Berti 2009: 190–1 for the confusion between *phronesis* and practical science in many contemporary philosophies. This confusion broadens the chasm between theoretical and practical realms.

## CHAPTER ONE

1 For good summaries of this story see Rorty 1982 and Putnam 1994, 221–44.
2 The best report for this history of surviving is probably the series of interviews with important characters of that story, "Let Me Tell You a Story: Heroes and Events of Pragmatism," which the *European*

*Journal of Pragmatism and American Philosophy* began publishing in July 2014.

3 See Rorty 1979.

4 Critics have often argued that pragmatists were Kant's followers, at least partially. This was not only because of Peirce's explicit statements, but also on the basis of more complex analysis. For instance, G. Mathur (1955) argues that James and Schiller were more Kantian than they admitted while still acknowledging their different conceptions of the "thing-in-itself." As will be seen, these interpretations do not capture the reiterated criticism and pragmatists' deep basic attitude.

5 Rorty's famous criticism, in fact, misses the participation of Peirce in the anti-Kantian perspective and does not actually enter into classic pragmatists' criticism of Kant.

6 Cf. Augustine 1970.

7 For different interpretation of the pattern of abduction see the volume of *Semiotica* 153, no. 1–4 (2005). In the same volume is my interpretation. For a more recent account, see Maddalena 2011.

8 See Zalamea 2001, Moore 2007a and 2007b, Havenel 2008, Maddalena 2009, 193–224.

9 For Peirce's manuscripts I will follow the indications of Robin Catalogue (1967).

10 Obviously, Johnston thinks that Dewey did not understand the difference and that Kant would have resolved the gap left by the first edition of the *Critique of Pure Reason* with the concept of noumenon, as a pure limit concept. Interestingly, Peirce thinks that the concept of noumenon has worsened the situation, which was still plausible in the first edition.

11 Bergson can hardly be considered a pragmatist but he shared many insights and philosophical concerns with James. One of them is clearly his anti-Kantianism. In his *Essay on the Immediate Data of Consciousness*, Bergson criticizes intellectualism as well. The French philosopher censures Kant for failing to grasp the difference between space and time, and consequently the difference between material and memory. In fact, according to Bergson, Kant conceived time on the basis of – and in analogy with – space (Bergson 1910,

91–4; 232–6). In this way, the experiences of time and of its peculiar duration are incomprehensible. According to Bergson, the result is the intellectualism he criticized with James and – similar to what Dewey said later – a separation between morality and nature, which makes them both incomprehensible. The separation between the reality of things in themselves and the "I" phenomenon is sanctioned by the intuitions of time and space. Uniformly designed, they settle "the thing itself" in an impossible metaphysics and phenomena in an alleged science able to analytically grasp reality in a sole "universal mathematics" (Bergson 1912, 71), a false security that only returns the frame of reality.

12 See Maddalena 2009b.

13 There should be a separate discussion on externalism, because it is true that it could not be unanimously shared by pragmatists; however, it is strongly affirmed by some and it persistently emerges in others, such as James, who seems to be contrary. James actually speaks of "retrospection" suggesting more retroductive inference than an intuitive principle.

14 For Peirce's scholastic realism see Boler 1963, Fisch 1967, Haack 1992, Mayorga 2007, Maddalena 2008.

15 See Margolis 2010.

16 See Maddalena 2014.

17 See Parravicini 2012. The quarrel between Peirce and Chauncey Wright about the entanglement of Mill's nominalism-evolutionism and criticism of Darwin by Peirce (*CP* 5.64) are very emblematic of this different view of evolution brought by pragmatism (*CP* 6.293–5).

18 See Lane 1997 and 1999.

19 One for all, are methods of inquiry and reasoning subject to change over time? Peirce does not ask and does not answer this question that would determine a more or less naturalist view of his thought.

## CHAPTER TWO

1 Brent 1998 is obviously one of the best sources to understand Peirce's critical conditions in his later years. But Fisch's archive

at the Peirce Project (Indianapolis) and the James-Peirce correspondence are a necessary complement to Brent's biography.

2 On the difficulty of really finding the "proof of pragmatism" see the classic paper by Max Fisch (Fisch 1986, 362–75). See also Christopher Hookway's many articles on the subject, in particular Hookway 2005. You can find a good hypothesis that connects the proof of pragmatism to existential graphs in Zalamea and Nubiola 2011.

3 Thomas L. Short calls the difficulties Peirce had to face "flaws." I do not think that there is a real discontinuity between "On A New List of Categories" and the following developments of Peirce's thought.

4 These topics appear as Peirce's research initiatives at different times in the years around the turn of the century: continuity (1898 Cambridge Conferences and 1903 Lowell Lectures), phaneroscopy (*EP2*, 360–70; *NEM4*, 320), signs (1903 Harvard Lectures), existential graphs (1903 Lowell Lectures), kinds of reasoning (*CP* 4.530–72), normative sciences (*EP2*, 371–97).

5 See Maddalena 2004.

6 *CPR* A7, B11: "In all judgments in which we think the relation of a subject to the predicate ... this relation is possible in two ways. Either the predicate B belongs to the subject A as something that is (covertly) contained in this concept A; or B, though connected with concept A, lies quite outside it. In the first case I call the judgment *analytic*; in the second, *synthetic*."

7 See Quine 1951, Kripke 1980.

8 "We saw, moreover, that the only way in which objects can be given to us is by modification of our sensibility; and, finally, that pure a priori concepts, besides containing the function of understanding implicit in the category, must also a priori contain formal conditions of sensibility (of inner sense specifically), conditions comprising the universal condition under which alone the category can be applied to any object. Let us call this formal and pure condition of sensibility, to which the concept of understanding is restricted in its use, the *schema* of this concept of understanding; and let us call the understanding's procedure with these *schemata* the schematism of pure understanding" (*CPR* 212, A 140, B179).

9 "To define, as the term itself yields, is in fact intended to mean no more than to exhibit a thing's comprehensive concept originally within its bounds" (*CPR* 679, A728, B756).

10 As a matter of fact, Peirce understands Kant's epistemic view as the one represented in the *Critique of Pure Reason*. In my opinion this is part of the analytic stand Peirce's philosophy took. Was Kant really reaching a different path of reasoning through the *Critique of Judgment*? Everything seems to indicate the opposite, but it is of course a possible alternative reading. However, Peirce did not think so (cf. Kaag 2005, 515–40).

11 See also (Gava 2014, 70–2). Gava pinpoints Peirce's phrase but solves the problem of syntheticity in Peirce's thought by referring to abductive reasoning. We are going to see that the picture of syntheticity is much more articulated.

12 It is indeed plausible to think of Peirce's logical project about synthetic reasoning as a kind of schematism (of course in a realist and not in a nominalist general comprehension) (cf. Rosenthal 2002). Peirce himself seems to appreciate the synthetic power of schematism when he says: "His doctrine of the schemata can only have been an afterthought, an addition to his system after it was substantially complete. For if schemata had been considered early enough, they would have overgrown his whole work" (*CP* 1.35).

13 See ch. 1, section 1.

14 Now by a logical analysis of an inference or proposition or concept, Peirce meant a dissection (*MS* 498) or a picking to pieces (*CP* 4.622) of the structure of that subject matter. And when he introduced EG to his audience at the Lowell Institute in 1903, he made clear at the start that the purpose the system was designed to fulfill was "to enable us to separate reasoning in its smallest steps so that each one may be examined by itself" (Roberts 1973, 110–11).

15 See Fisch 1986, 261–82, Colapietro 2004.

16 The three degrees of clarity are stated in "How To Make Our Ideas Clear" (*W2*, 257–76). For the fourth degree see (*EP2*, 255). See also (Nubiola 2009) for other occurrences of the word.

## CHAPTER THREE

1 Cf. Maddalena 2006.

2 The history of contemporary mathematics and a valid proposal of a consequent philosophical shift is argued by Zalamea 2008, chs 1 and 3.

3 Brandom singles out the problem of syntheticity in Kant. His reading stresses that "understanding is something that we do" (1994, 80), where "doing" means "synthetizing." However, his project is fully inscribed in the Kantian and analytic paradigms. In fact, Brandom wants to "make explicit" what practices say in their performances and not to revise Kant's description of synthesis allowing performances to be part of reasoning. Playing with words, we could say that the project of my book could be described as "making it implicit." Given the characteristics listed in ch. 1, it is difficult even to accept Brandom's project as part of pragmatism. In particular, the way to look at representation and continuity separates it from the legacy of classic pragmatism. Because of the broad and well-developed interest raised by Brandom's project, a careful comparison with it would be important in further steps of the "philosophy of gesture."

4 The distinction of substantive and transitive parts is in *The Principles of Psychology* (James 1975, 243).

5 Peirce made semiotics coincide with logic insofar as the latter is normally understood (*CP* 1.444). The paradigm we are developing makes this insight more clear.

6 For scholarly studies on this topic see both Moore 2007a and Maddalena 2009, 137–92.

7 The chronology of changes is now well established. For the latest solutions see Havenel 2008 and Maddalena 2009, 193–24. The genesis of Peirce's continuum is well explained by Moore 2007, and its possible mathematical development by Zalamea 2001.

8 Zalamea subsumes transitivity under modality (2001, 51–75) but I prefer to make it a general character of Peirce's continuum because of the fundamental role of transitivity in explaining "change."

9 Cantor held a similar view in distinguishing the "infinite" as a mathematical object from the "absolute infinite"; see Purkert

1988, 49–66. I will not discuss the ontological issue in this book. It deserves a more careful examination that will occupy several years of research.

10 Peirce states the same difference between mathematics and logic – and also stressed the primeval role of mathematics for logic – in the third Lowell Lecture (*MS* 458, 4).

11 This foundation of mathematics on our "doing mathematics" also implies an a posteriori foundation of mathematics that changes the comprehension of the relationship among analytic, a priori, and necessary, and agrees with Kripke's fundamental assessments on the same topic.

12 For the use of *de dicto* and *de re* necessities in Peirce see Lane 1997.

13 A good example of vagueness is the spontaneous belief in God. And a good example of the support that abductive inference receives from vagueness is shown by the idea of God in "A Neglected Argument for the Reality of God" (*EP2*, 434–50).

14 For the many occurrences of the concept of concrete reasonableness see also Nubiola 2009.

15 For this distinction, see Ricoeur 2005.

16 This is a common feeling shared by almost the entire community of scholars of pragmatism. One of the most recent and valid contributions comes from Margolis 2010.

17 See also Shin 2002, 13–35.

18 As is well known, icons, indices, and symbols represent the relationship with the dynamic object. Here I will not elaborate further the classification of signs and of objects because what we need at this point is only to understand that the more basic iconic level has often been discarded by logicians, losing that original "evidence" Peirce was seeking with EG.

19 I have to thank Fernando Zalamea for this insight. He fully develops a mathematical and philosophical presentation of EG in Zalamea 2010.

20 For a complete explanation, see Short 2007, 264–70.

21 Technically speaking, the loose end arises from the rule of erasure and iteration that "permits a branch with a loose end to be added to or retracted from any line of identity" (*CP* 4.505).

22 Peirce explains this difference by referring to the difference between grapheus – to whom the world we have to represent is already an

actual existent – and graphist (or logician) to whom the world is possible or necessary but not yet actual (*CP* 4.431).

23 "A Line of Identity that abuts upon a Cut, whereas on its Area or on its Place may *look* alike at its two ends; but an essential part of every diagram is the Conventions by which it is interpreted; and the principle that Graphs are Endoporeutic in interpretation, as they naturally will be in the process of scribing, confers a definite *sens*, as the French say, a definite way of facing, a definite front and back, to the Line" (*NEM* 4, 329).

24 Peirce defines "aspect" as "the word which I propose to use as the technical designation of a qualisign that is so related to a sinsign." "So related" means that a qualisign may be a "fluctuating inconsistent memory of a sinsign, namely of a definite individual existent which is significant because of the circumstances of its existence" (*MS* 284, 65–6).

25 For the problem of the form in a general reconstruction of Peirce's semiotic see Liszka 1996, 20–4.

26 Here comes also the problem of misrecognition. This is not the place to analyze it, but the fundamental logic of misrecognition remains the same, while its value changes (it is a recognition later recognized as imperfect – "recognizability and being are almost synonymous terms" (*EP* 1, 25).

27 Peirce criticized this view: "For this error is, with one exception, the most fatal of all those into which great minds have ever fallen" (*MS* 659, 38).

28 For this critique of Hegel it is important also to look at the work of the so-called "second Schelling" and at his positive philosophy.

## CHAPTER FOUR

1 See Zalamea 2012; Cavaillès 1994; Châtelet 1993 and 2010.

2 Studies on gestures have also been undertaken in recent psychological and sociological research. A good guide to a history of studies on gestures from antiquity to present times is in Kendon 2004. This careful history and Kendon's proposal show that "gesture" has always been considered as "utterance uses of visible action" (Kendon 2004, 1–2). The importance of gesture as an

"attempt to give information of some sort" (ibid., 7) emerges also from these studies. However, the consideration of gesture is limited to body movements somehow related to the signification of words. It is a long history in which gestures have been read as primitive or parallel forms of language. Here I will consider gesture as a completion of reasoning and communication in which words can cooperate. This view is much broader than a bodily articulation: (complete) gestures are the original form of reasoning from which all other forms – language included – derive. It is a philosophical reading of gesture, a vision at which sometimes authors of the history told by Kendon hinted. This perspective also opens up a new way to look at body gestures, furnishing a better pattern to the admirable studies that have been carried out. Another wonderful reconstruction that covers the history of gesture in Antiquity and the Middle Ages is in Schmitt 1990. Schmitt observes that during the Middle Ages gestures had been described, above all by Hugh of Saint Victor, as effective signs moved by an aesthetic *figuratio*. Our semiotic pattern will give a better account to this insight.

3 See Maddalena 2014.

4 Mead's idea that an index extrapolates a character from a gesture is fully respected here. See also Mead 1934, 95. My view agrees with Mead on many points, above all in considering language as a particular kind of gesture. However, this view gives a logical foundation in continuity and a semiotic definition of gestures to Mead's insight.

5 I hope in this way to render justice to very powerful insights of authors like MacIntyre (1981), Taylor (1988), and Colapietro (2006).

6 See Dewey 1934.

7 By this term Peirce named the study of the elements of sign.

8 Peirce scholars agree on the fundamental importance of teleology but they often argue on the correct interpretation of it. For two different comprehensive views see Short 2007, 117–77, Hulswit 2002, 133–66, and Gava 2014, 112–14. I agree with Gava's general interpretation, which sees Peirce's metaphysics as "dependent on his purposeful account of thought and sign process" (Gava 2014, 2). However, I do not think that this characteristic is a sufficient

reason not to admit that Peirce was abandoning Kant's picture of epistemology over the years.

9 Private conversation, Bogotà, 29–30 August 2013.

10 There are important connections between this semiotic view and mathematical topological studies as Riemann's surfaces.

11 A more complex discourse is deserved by the role of vagueness that cannot be the topic of this book.

12 See Maddalena 2006.

13 This description concerns the entire kind of reasoning within the new paradigm. Therefore, the term "familiar" is here taken in a different sense from the usual and the Wittgensteinian use that we listed as "schematization." In fact, we are not talking here only about the phenomenological or semiotic aspect of an action but of the kind of reasoning as such.

14 See Maddalena and Zalamea 2012.

## CHAPTER FIVE

1 For this reading of abduction based on an aesthetical and ethical reading of signs see Maddalena 2005 and 2011, but also Anderson 1987.

2 Liszka commented on a first draft of this chapter at the XIV Conference on Pragmatism in São Paulo, Brazil, 5–8 November 2012.

3 The completely synthetic pattern also includes what Cavell sees as a third way – neither descriptive nor normative – to learn the world and the language together accounting for meaning and reasonableness implicit in our assertion (1969).

4 Cf. ch. 3, section 2.2.

5 Paradoxically, this view overlaps Aquinas' on the difference between the behaviour of essence and existence in God and human beings.

6 Psycho-sociological studies on body gestures share the same conviction, which I think is unavoidable. "There is always the implication that the actor is deemed to exercise at least some degree of voluntary control over any movement regarded as 'gesture' and what it expresses" (Kendon 2004, 8).

7 Cf. Calcaterra 2003, 43–56.

8 See Maddalena 2010a.
9 Cf. T.S. Eliot 1922.
10 Cf. *EP2*, 253–5.
11 See Potter 1967.

## CHAPTER SIX

1 The proposed philosophy hints toward a curious kind of a posteriori foundation, similar to the one that we have to ascribe to mathematics when we read it through a Peircean lens. The topic of the metaphysical import is quite difficult and needs studies that I do not intend to carry out through this book. However, the theses that I present in this book already imply a very strong sort of metaphysical realism that Peirce himself pursued, even though adherence to realism does not predetermine which face this realism should have.
2 Kruijff 2005, Maddalena 2005, Nubiola 2005.
3 Colapietro 1989, 2004, 2006; Ricoeur 1993, 244–57, 2005; MacIntyre 1981; Taylor 1989. The account given by Colapietro (2006) is obviously and by far the closest to the one I advocate here. Similar to Colapietro, I think that a "pragmatist form of reflective acknowledgment" is the way to identity that Peirce's works suggest. Colapietro's powerful reading illuminates the way we can use Peirce's description of taking habit and of historical involvement and development. I tried to figure out the logic of acknowledgment in a path different from the analytic one, using the tools Peirce forged (such as the idea of "habit") but putting them in a different account of rationality. Interestingly, when MacIntyre proposes his ideas of practice (MacIntyre 1981, 181–225), he has to tackle the same topic of personal identity in order to explain what that tool means. This chapter faces the same task.
4 "True continuity" is the term Peirce used to indicate the continuity that eludes the calculations of set theory. See ch. 3, section 1.
5 See ch. 3, section 2.
6 Usually we define this property of narrations saying that we belong to a tradition. For a reading of Peirce in this direction see again Colapietro (2004, 2006). Colapietro and Cavell (1969, 44–72)

also understand the second part of Wittgenstein's thought as recognizing this kind of belonging to a tradition. Of course you can read Wittgenstein the other way around as Kripke does (1982). It depends on how you read the ultimate justification provided by "forms of life" (Wittgenstein 1953, 226) or "conventions" (Wittgenstein 1958, 24). I find them both plausible. Skipping this difficult debate, I understand that Wittgenstein's familiarity with meaning does not coincide with Peirce's "taking habit" but rather with Peirce's first, familiar degree of clarity of an idea. My description of complete gestures tells us that familiar meaning is the kind of habit that has lost or not yet achieved its completion (the actual blending of different signs), and therefore according to the proposed list it becomes or remains schematic or repetitive. The understandability of ourselves within a tradition is a point also made clear by MacIntyre (204–25).

7 I will use this example as a literary report without entering the discussion about its historical truth.

8 See ch. 4, section 1.

9 See Niño 2007 and Maddalena 2009, 57–78.

10 For my interpretation of abduction, see ch. 1, section 1.

11 I am grateful for this suggestion to Vincent Colapietro.

12 See note 5.

13 See ch. 3, section 3.

14 Cf. Ricoeur 2005.

15 See ch. 5, section 3.

## CHAPTER SEVEN

1 For the story of the manuscript and the entire work of recognition of Grossman's writing, see the website of the Vasily Grossman Study Center, www.grossmanweb.eu

2 Of course, one of the notable exceptions is Hannah Arendt's work on totalitarianism (1951).

3 See Bonola 2007.

4 See ch. 5, section 2.

## CHAPTER EIGHT

1 See ch. 5, section 3.

2 In my reconstruction abduction is the top application of this mixing: abduction formulates hypotheses reading signs from an aesthetical and ethical point of view (Maddalena 2009, 57–78). See ch. 5, section 2.3.

3 See Maddalena 2003, 99–101, about *MS* 678.

4 See Dewey 1925, 239; James 1904a; *EP2*, 2–3.

5 See Calcaterra 2005, which is totally dedicated to this pragmatist view of selfhood.

6 See Hookway 2011.

7 See ch. 1, section 1.

8 Here I use the term "dogma" not in the technical Catholic sense of the word.

9 We should underline the difference between repetition and copy. A repetition (like repeating by heart) is still an incomplete gesture that is able to synthetize even if in a limited measure. In repetition icons are weak but not absent. Copies are not gestures anymore because of the total lack of iconicity.

10 See ch. 7, section 1.

11 This view is contrary to what Umberto Eco says in his *Trattato di semiotica* (1975) where he denies the role of the dynamic object as resistant to interpretation. Eco himself corrected his position in *Kant e l'ornitorinco* (Eco 1997).

12 Josiah Royce's *Philosophy of Loyalty* is an interesting pragmatist attempt to look at ethics strictly understood. Loyalty is both practical and theoretical – that is, it is an embodied morality. It requires both individual and tradition; it respects common sense evolutionist values; it increases by training. Somehow, loyalty is indifferent to the goodness of the cause to which one is loyal. Only the internal growth of loyalty would eventually discriminate among loyalties. The philosophy of gesture is the phenomenological/semiotic structure that Royce's idea admittedly was not thought to have (2005, 857). A closer study of the relationship between philosophies of gesture and loyalty could be worth pursuing.

However, other ethical (and political) perspectives could be also proposed and fostered starting from the structure of gestures.

13 This is of course a new way to look at the concept of "practice" used by MacIntyre (1981). There is also a teleological part in complete gesture, but this part is not completely pre-constituted by history and tradition. The complete gesture itself can be the place in which a new understanding of the aim appears. Moreover, the actual-existential and the possible-iconic parts make understandable the relationship between the aim and the experience from which the complete gesture rises.

14 See Maddalena 2009, 79–96.

15 See also Calcaterra (2005).

16 See figure 4.2 at p. 77

17 Two important suggestions must be raised here. 1) Our paradigm is aligned with the pragmatist tradition that finds in Mead's "taking role" an important explanation of this phenomenon. Moreover, it grants that this taking role does not have to find any sort of foundation in "sympathy" or "empathy." Re-performance is simply an externalist way to repeat gestures. It is the phenomenological and semiotic nature of gesture itself to grant the transmission of meaning. 2) The contemporary attention to different educational tools such as cooperative learning, tutoring, and role playing show that the tool of complete gestures is somehow foreseen by the educational system. The focus on it and the comprehension of its dynamic structure will help these attempts, providing a guide to which elements have to be respected and ameliorated.

18 Recent discoveries about mirror-neurons show that the mind is sensitive to gestures (Rizzolatti and Sinigaglia 2008). This sensitivity is so strong that it responds to them not only when the subject does something, but also when the subject sees others doing something. This discovery proves for phenomenologists and for pragmatists that universals are communicated through gestures. In our reading, though, what is properly human is the capacity to recognize identity through changes – to synthetize or to embody the universal meaning into different circumstances by complete gestures. In any case, the rational pattern based on the tool of complete gesture seems to go

along with this recent discovery, and to strengthen and specify its insights.

19 In the same pragmatist tradition see the important critique by Mead (1934, 51–60).

20 See also Costa 2010, 77–8.

21 *Measure for Measure*, act 2, sc. 2, l. 117–22.

## CONCLUSIONS AND FURTHER STUDIES

1 A significant three year's project (2011–14) "Pourquoi le pragmatism? L'intérêt du pragmatisme pour les sciences humaines et sociales" about pragmatism and sociology was carried on at Villa Vigoni under the lead of Tanja Bogusz, Roberto Frega, Albert Ogien. A promising Peircean understanding of semiotics is followed by (Gili and Colombo 2012) in their handbook on communication. Valentina Mazzoni (Verona, Italy) and Oscar Zelis (Buenos Aires, Argentina) have already developed some significant studies partially using the philosophy of gesture in pedagogy and psychology respectively.

# References


Alighieri, Dante. 1991. *Commedia*. Edited by A.M. Chiavacci Leonardi. Milano: Mondadori.

Anderson, Douglas R. 1987. Creativity and the Philosophy of C.S. Peirce. Dordrecht: Martinus Nijhoff.

Arendt, Hannah. 1951. *The Origins of Totalitarianism*. Cleveland: World Pub. Co.

– 1963. *Eichmann in Jerusalem*. New York: Viking Penguin.

Auerbach, Erich. 2007 (1929). *Dante: Poet of the Secular World*. Translated by Ralph Manheim. New York: nyrb Classics.

Augustine, Aurelius. 1970. *Contra Academicos*. Edited by V. Tarulli. Roma: Città Nuova.

Bergson, Henri. 1910. *Time and Free Will: An Essay on the Immediate Data of Consciousness*. Translated by F.L. Pogson. New York: MacMillan.

– 1912. *An Introduction to Metaphysics*. Translated by T.E. Hulme. New York: Putnam's Sons.

Berti, Enrico. 2009. "Alasdair MacIntyre: comunità e tradizione." In *Sperare nell'uomo*, edited by G. Chiosso, 177–95. Torino: SEI.

Boler, John F. 1963. *Charles Peirce and Scholastic Realism*. Seattle: University of Washington Press.

Bonola, Anna. 2007. "Discorso totalitario e dissenso linguistico in *Vita e destino* di Vasilij Grossman." In *Il romanzo della libertà. Vasilij Grossman tra i classici del XX secolo*, edited by G. Maddalena and P. Tosco, 89–129. Soveria Mannelli (CZ): Rubbettino.

Brandom, Robert B. 1994. *Making It Explicit: Reasoning Representing, and Discursive Commitment*. Cambridge: Harvard University Press.
– 2011. *Perspectives on Pragmatism*. Cambridge: Harvard University Press.
Brent, Joseph. 1998 (1993). *C.S. Peirce: A Life*. Indianapolis and Bloomington: Indiana University Press.
Calcaterra, Rosa M. 2003. *Pragmatismo: I valori dell'esperienza. Letture di Peirce, James e Mead*. Roma: Carocci.
– (ed.) 2005. *Semiotica e fenomenologia del Sé*. Torino: Aragno.
Carpenter, Humphrey (ed.). 1995. *The Letters of J.R.R. Tolkien*. London: Harper and Collins.
Cavaillès, Jean. 1994. *Œuvres complètes*. Paris : Hermann.
Châtelet, Gilles. 1993. *Les enjeux du mobile*. Paris : Éditions du Seuil.
– 2010. *L'enchantement du virtuel*. Edited by C. Alunni and C. Paoletti. Paris: Éditions Rue d'Ulm.
Chauviré, Christiane. 2008. *L'oeil mathématique. Essai sur la philosophie mathematique de Peirce*. Paris: Éditions Kimé.
Chevalier, Jean M. 2013. "Peirce's Critique of the First Critique: a Leibnizian False Start." *Transactions of the Charles S. Peirce Society* 49 (1): 1–26.
Colapietro, Vincent M. 2004. "Putting Peirce's Doctrine of Interpretants to work." *Semiotiche* 1: 49–68.
– 2006. "Toward a Pragmatic Conception of Practical Identity." *Transactions of the Charles S. Peirce Society* 42, no. 2: 173–205.
– 2013. "Time as Experience/Experience as Temporality: Pragmatic and Perfectionist Reflections on Extemporaneous Creativity." *European Journal of Pragmatism and American Philosophy* 5, no. 1: 77–101.
Costa, Vincenzo. 2010. *Fenomenologia dell'intersoggettività*. Roma: Carocci.
De Tienne, André. 2000. "Quand l'apparence (se) fait signe: la genèse de la représentation chez Peirce." *RS/SI* 20: 95–144.
– 2004. "Is Phaneroscopy as a Pre-semiotic Science Possible?" *Semiotiche* 2: 15–30.
– 2005. "La persona come segno." In *Semiotica e fenomenologia del Sé*, edited by R.M. Calcaterra, 91–109. Torino: Aragno.
– 2009. "Preface." In Maddalena, Giovanni. *Metafisica per assurdo*, VII–XXV. Soveria Mannelli: Rubbettino.

Dewey, John. 1981 (1925). *Experience and Nature*. In *The Collected Works of John Dewey, 1882–1953. Later Works*, vol. 1 (*LW1*). Carbondale and Edwardsville: Southern Illinois University Press.

– 1985 (1932). *Ethics*. In *The Collected Works of John Dewey, 1882–1953. Later Works*, vol. 7 (*LW7*). Carbondale and Edwardsville: Southern Illinois University Press.

– 1986 (1933). "Essays and How to Think, Revised Edition." In *The Collected Works of John Dewey, 1882–1953. Later Works, vol. 8. (LW8)*. Carbondale and Edwardsville: Southern Illinois University Press.

– 1989 (1934). *Art as Experience*. In *The Collected Works of John Dewey, 1882–1953. Later Works*, vol. 10 (*LW10*). Carbondale and Edwardsville: Southern Illinois University Press.

Eco, Umberto. 1975. *Trattato di semiotica generale*. Milan: Bompiani.

– 1997. *Kant e l'ornitorinco*. Milan: Bompiani

Fisch, Max H. 1967. "Peirce's Progress from Nominalism toward Realism." *The Monist* 51, no. 2: 159–78.

– 1986. *Peirce, Semeiotic and Pragmatism: Essays by Max H. Fisch*. Edited by K. Ketner and C. Kloesel. Bloomington: Indiana Univesity Press.

Formis, Barbara. 2010. *Esthétique de la vie ordinaire*. Paris: PUF

Frege, Gottlob. 1980 (3rd edition). *Philosophical Writings of Gottlob Frege*. Edited by P. Geach and M. Black. London: Basil Blackwell.

Gadamer, Hans-Georg. 1960. *Wahrheit und Methode: Grundzüge einer Philosophischen Hermeneutiken*. Tübingen: Mohr.

Garrard, John, and Carol Garrard. 2012. *The Life and Fate of Vasily Grossman*. London: Pen and Sword.

Gava, Gabriele. 2014. *Peirce's Account of Purposefulness: A Kantian Perspective*. New York: Routledge.

Gili, Guido, and Fausto Colombo. 2012. *Comunicazione, cultura e società: un approccio sociologico alla relazione comunicativa*. Brescia: La scuola.

Gingerich, Owen. 2011. "Kepler and the Laws of Nature." *Euresis Journal* 1: 9–16.

Giussani, Luigi. 1998. *At the Origin of Christian Claim*. Montreal: McGill University Press.

Grossman, Vasily. 2010. *The Road*. Edited by R. and E. Chandler. London: Maclehose Press.

– 2011. *Life and Fate*. London: Vintage 2011.

James, William. 1975 (1890). *Principles of Psychology*. Cambridge: Harvard University Press.

– 1978 (1895). "The Knowing of Things Together," in *Essays in Philosophy*. Edited by F. Burkhardt, F. Bowers, I.K. Skrupskelis, 71–89. Cambridge: Harvard University Press.

– 1912 (1896). *The Will to Believe*. London: Longsman, Green & Co.

– 1961 (1902). *The Varieties of Religious Experience*. New York: MacMillian.

– 1904. "The Pragmatic Method." *The Journal of Philosophy Psychology and Scientific Method* 26, no. 1: 673–87.

– 1904a. "Does Consciousness Exist." *The Journal of Philosophy Psychology and Scientific Method* 1: 477–91.

– 1916 (1907). *Pragmatism*. London: Longsman, Green & Co.

– 1909. *A Pluralistic Universe*. London: Longsman, Green & Co.

– 1997 (1911). *The Meaning of Truth*. New York: Prometheus Books.

Johnston, James S. 2006. "Dewey's Critique of Kant." *Transactions of the Charles S. Peirce Society* 42, no. 4: 518–51.

Haack, Susan. 1992. "Extreme Scholastic Realism: Its Relevance to Philosophy of Science Today." *Transactions of the Charles S. Peirce Society* 28 (1): 19–50.

– 2009. *Evidence and Inquiry*. Amherst: Prometheus Books.

Hanna, Robert. 2001. *Kant and the Foundations of Analytic Philosophy*. Oxford: Clarendon Press.

Havenel, Jérôme. 2008. "Peirce's Clarifications on Continuity." *Transactions of Charles S. Peirce Society* 44, no. 1: 86–133.

Homer. 2009. *The Odyssey of Homer*. Translated by R. Lattimore. New York: Harper Collins.

Hookway, Christopher. 2005. "The Pragmatist Maxim and the Proof of Pragmatism." *Cognitio* (9): 25–42.

– 2011. "James's Epistemology and the Will to Believe." *European Journal of Pragmatism and American Philosophy* 3 (1): 30–8.

Hulswit, Menno. 2002. *From Cause to Causation: A Peircean Perspective*. Dordrecht: Keuwer Academic Publisher.

Kaag, John. 2005. "Continuity and Inheritance: Kant's Critique of Judgment and the Work of C.S. Peirce." *Transactions of Charles S. Peirce Society* 41 (3): 515–40.

Kant, Immanuel. 1996 (1781–87). *Critique of Pure Reason: Unified Edition*. Indianapolis, Cambridge: Hackett Publishing Company.

– 1898. *Critique of Practical Reason*. London: Longsman and Green.

Kendon, Adam. 2004. *Gesture: Visible Action as Utterance*. Cambridge: Cambridge University Press.

Kripke, Saul. 1980. *Naming and Necessity*. Cambridge: Harvard University Press.

– 1982. *Wittgenstein on Rules and Private Language*. Cambridge: Harvard University Press.

Kruijff, Gert-Jan. 2005. "Peirce's Late Theory of Abduction. A Comprehensive Account." *Semiotica* 153, no. 1–4: 431–54.

Lane, Robert. 1997. "Peirce's 'Entanglement' with the Principles of Excluded Middle and Contradiction." *Transactions of the Charles S. Peirce Society* 33, no. 3: 680–703.

– 1999. "Peirce's Triadic Logic Revisited." *Transactions of the Charles S. Peirce Society* 35, no. 2: 284–311.

Levinas, Emmanuel. 1961. *Totalité et Infini. Essai sur l'exteriorité*. La Haye: M. Nijhoff.

Lewis, David. 1976. "Survival and Identity." In *The Identities of Persons*, edited by A. Rorty, 12–47. California: Berkeley.

Liszka, James J. 1996. *A General Introduction to the Semiotic of Charles Sanders Peirce*. Indianapolis and Bloomington: Indiana University Press.

Longo, Giuseppe. 2015. "La conseguenze della filosofia." In *Esercizio de equilibrio in filosofia*. Edited by R. Laufredini. Pisa: ETS.

MacIntyre, Alasdair. 1981. *After Virtue: A Study in Moral Theory*. Notre Dame: University of Notre Dame Press.

– 1988. *Whose Justice? Which Rationality?* Notre Dame: University of Notre Dame Press.

– 1990. Three Rival Versions of Moral Enquiry: Encyclopaedia, Genealogy, Tradition. Notre Dame: University of Notre Dame Press.

– 1999. Dependent Rational Animals. Why Human Beings Need the Virtues. Chicago and La Salle: Open Court.

Maddalena, Giovanni. 2004. "Peirce and Cantor on Metaphysical Realism." *Semiotiche* 1: 137–48.

– 2005. "Abduction and Metaphysical Realism." *Semiotica* 153, no. 1–4: 243–59.

– 2006. "Peirce, Proper Names and Nicknames." In *Semiotics and Philosophy in Charles Sanders Peirce*, edited by R. Fabbrichesi and S. Marietti, 22–35. Newcastle: Cambridge Scholars Press.

– 2008. "Un estremista dello scotismo: Charles S. Peirce." *Quaestio: annuario di storia della metafisica* 8: 569–84.

– 2009. *Metafisica per assurdo*. Soveria Mannelli: Rubbettino.

– 2009b. "L'attualità dell'anti-kantismo di Vailati." *Cent'anni di Giovanni Vailati*. Edited by I. Pozzoni, 293–306. Milano: Liminamentis.

– 2010. "Peirce and Vailati on Semiotics and Freedom." *Cognitio* 11: 58–68.

– 2010a. "Peirce's Theory of Assent." In *Ideas in Action*, edited by M. Bergman, A.V. Pietarinen, H. Rydenfelt, and S. Paavola, 211–23. Helsinki: Nordic Studies in Pragmatism.

– 2011. "Guessing or Reasoning? A Philosophical Account of Hypothesis." *Euresis Journal* 1: 29–44.

– 2014. *Conoscere e rappresentare*. Torino: Heritage Club.

Maddalena, Giovanni, and Fernando Zalamea. 2012. "A New Analytic/Synthetic/Horotic Paradigm. From Mathematical Gesture to Synthetic/Horotic Reasoning." *European Journal of Pragmatism and American Philosophy* 6: 208–24 .

Marchetti, Sarin. 2012. "James, l'etica e la teoria morale." In *Pragmata. Per una ricostruzione storiografica dei Pragmatismi*, edited by I. Pozzoni, 57–86. Morolo: if Press.

– 2012b. "James e l'etica." In *Pragmatismi*, edited by I. Pozzoni, 81–134. Milano: Limina Mentis.

Margolis, Joseph. 1999. *What, After All, Is a Work of Art? Lectures in the Philosophy of Art*. University Park: Pennsylvania State University Press.

– 2010. *Pragmatism's Advantage*. Stanford: Stanford University Press.

Mathur, George. 1955. "Hume and Kant in Their Relation to the Pragmatic Movement." *Journal of the History of Ideas* 16, no. 2: 198–208.

Mayorga, Rosa M. 2007. *From Realism to "Realicism." The Metaphysics of Charles Sanders Peirce*. Lankam: Lexington Books.

Mead, George H. 1932. *The Philosophy of the Present*. Chicago: The Open Court.

– 1936. *Movements of Thought in the Nineteenth Century*. Chicago: The University of Chicago Press.

– 1972 (1934). *Mind, Self, and Society*. Chicago and London: University of Chicago Press.

Merleau-Ponty, Maurice. 1988 (1953). *In Praise of Philosophy*. Evanston: Northwestern University Press.

Misak, Cheryl. 2013 *The American Pragmatists*. Oxford: Oxford University Press.

Moore, Matthew E. 2007a. "On Peirce's Discovery of Cantor's Theorem." *Cognitio* 8, no. 2: 223–48.

– 2007b. "The Genesis of the Peircean Continuum." *Transactions of the Charles S. Peirce Society* 43, no. 3: 425–69.

Newman, John H. 1973. *An Essay in Aid of a Grammar of Assent*. Westminster: Christian Classics Inc.

Niño, Douglas. 2007. "Abducting Abduction. Avatares sobre la comprensión de la Abducción de Charles S. Peirce." PhD dissertation, Universidad Nacional de Colombia, Bogotà.

Nozick, Robert. 1981. *Philosophical Explanations*. Cambridge: Harvard University Press.

Nubiola, Jaime. 2009. "What Reasonableness Really Is." *Transactions of the Charles S. Peirce Society* 45 (2): 125–34.

Papini, Giovanni. 1906. *Il crepuscolo dei filosofi*. Milano: Società Editrice Lombarda.

Parfit, Derek. 1971. "Personal Identity." *Philosophical Review* 80: 3–27.

Parravicini, Andrea. 2012. Il pensiero in evoluzione. Chauncey Wright tra darwinismo e pragmatismo. Pisa: ets.

Peirce, Charles S. 1931–35. *Collected Papers* (CP). vols I–VI. Edited by P. Weiss e C. Hartshorne. Cambridge: Harvard University Press.

– 1958. *Collected Papers* (*CP*). vols VII–VIII. Edited by A.W. Burks. Cambridge: Harvard University Press.

– 1976. *The New Elements of Mathematics* (*NEM*). Edited by C. Eisele. The Hague: Mouton.

– 1977. *Semiotics and Significs: The Correspondence between Charles S. Peirce and Victoria Lady Welby.* Edited by C.S. Hardwick. Bloomington: Indian University Press.

– 1997. *Pragmatism as a Principle and a Method of Right Thinking. The 1903 Harvard Lectures on Pragmatism.* Edited by P.A. Turrisi. State University of New York Press, Albany.

– 1992. *The Essential Peirce*, vol. 1 (*EP1*). Edited by N. Houser and C. Kloesel. Bloomington and Indianapolis: Indiana University Press.

– 1998. *The Essential Peirce*, vol. 2 (*EP2*). Edited by The Peirce Edition Project. Bloomington-Indianapolis: Indiana University Press.

– 1998b. *Reasoning and the Logic of Things*. Edited by K. Ketner and H. Putnam. Cambridge: Harvard University Press.

– 1981–2010. *Writings of Charles Sanders Peirce* (*W*), vols 1–6, 8. Edited by The Peirce Edition Project. Bloomington-Indianapolis: Indiana University Press.

Plato. 2010. *Ion*. Boston: Actonian Press.

– 2000. *The Apology of Socrates*. Indianapolis: Hackett.

Potter, Vincent G. 1967. *Charles S. Peirce On Norms and Ideals.* Worcester: The University of Massachusetts.

Purkert, Walter. 1988. *Cantor's Views on the Foundations of Mathematics*. In *The History of Modern Mathematics*, edited by D.E. Rowe and J. McCleary, 49–66. London: Academic Press.

Putnam, Hilary. 1994. *Words and Life*. Cambridge: Harvard University Press.

Quine, W.V.O. 1951. "Two Dogmas of Empiricism." *The Philosophical Review* 60: 20–43.

Ricoeur, Paul. 2005. *The Course of Recognition*. Translated by D. Pellauer. Cambridge: Harvard University Press.

Rizzolatti, Giacomo, and Corrado Sinigaglia. 2008. *Mirrors in the Brain: How Our Minds Share Actions, Emotions, and Experience*. Oxford: Oxford University Press.

Roberts, Don D. 1973. *The Existential Graphs of Charles S. Peirce*. The Hague-Paris: Mouton.

Robin, Richard S. 1967. *Annotated Catalogue of the Papers of Charles S. Peirce*. Amherst: The University of Massachusetts Press.

Rorty, Richard. 1979. *Philosophy and the Mirror of Nature*. Princeton: Princeton University Press.

– 1982. *Consequences of Pragmatism*. Minneapolis: University of Minnesota Press.

Rosenthal, Sandra B. 2002. "A Pragmatic Appropriation of Kant. Lewis and Peirce." *Transactions of the Charles S. Peirce Society* 38, no. 1–2: 253–66.

Royce, Josiah. 2005 (1908). *The Philosophy of Loyalty*. In *Basic Writings*, edited by J.J. McDermott, 855–1014. New York: Fordham University Press.

Schiller, F.C.S. 2008 (1902). "Axioms as Postulates." In *Personal Idealism*, edited by H. Sturt, 32–103. London and New York: MacMillan. Now in F.C.S. Schiller, *On Pragmatism and Humanism. Selected Writings 1891–1939*. Edited by H.J.R. Shook and H.P. McDonald. Amherst: Prometheus Books.

Schmitt, Jean-Claude. 1990. *La raison des gestes dans l'Occident médiéval*. Paris: Éditions Gallimard.

Shin, Sun-Joo. 2002. *The Iconic Logic of Peirce's Graphs*. Cambridge: The MIT Press.

Shakespeare, William. 1997. *Measure for Measure*. In *The Riverside Shakespeare*, edited by G. Blakemore Evans et al., 49–66. Boston: Houghton, Mifflin Co.

Shoemaker, Sydney. 1984. "Personal Identity: A Materialist's Account." In *Personal Identity*. Edited by S. Shoemaker and R. Swinburne. Oxford: Blackwell.

Short, Thomas L. 2007. *Peirce's Theory of Signs*. Cambridge: Cambridge University Press.

Shusterman, Richard. 1992. *Pragmatist Aesthetics: Living Beauty, Rethinking Art*. Oxford: Blackwell.

Taylor, Charles. 1989. *Sources of the Self*. Cambridge: Cambridge University Press.

Tomasello, Michael. 1999. *The Cultural Origins of Human Cognition*. Cambridge: Harvard University Press.

Vailati, Giovanni. 1971. *Epistolario: 1891–1909*. Edited by G. Lanaro. Torino: Einaudi.

– 2003. *Gli strumenti della ragione*. Edited by M. Quaranta. Padova: il Poligrafo.

Wittgenstein, Ludwig. 1984. *Werkausgabe, Band I. Tractatus logico-philosophicus, Tagebücher 1914–1916, Philosophische Untersuchungen*. Frankfurt am Main: Suhrkamp.

Zalamea, Fernando. 2001. *El continuo Peirceano*. Facultad de Ciencias, Bogotà: Universidad Nacional de Colombia.

– 2008. *Filosofia sintetica de las matematicas contemporaneas*. Bogotà: Universidad Nacional de Colombia.

– 2010. *Los graficos existenciales peirceanos*. Bogotà: Universidad Nacional de Colombia.

– 2012. *Seminario Filosofía francesa de la matemática en el siglo XX*. Manuscripto.

Zalamea, Fernando, and Jaime Nubiola. 2011. "Existential Graphs and Proofs of Pragmatism." *Semiotica* 2011, no. 186: 412–39.

# Index